Palgrave Studies in Logistics and Supply Chain Management

Series Editors

Martin Christopher, School of Management, Cranfield University, Cranfield, Beds., UK
Emel Aktas, School of Management, Cranfield University, Cranfield, UK

Logistics and supply chain management has always been critical to business success and to the efficient running of economies and the well-being of the societies they serve. In recent years, however, the importance of these activities has been highlighted by geopolitical challenges and uncertainty that have threatened global supply chains.

The series provides an opportunity to explore in-depth and with rigour topics such as digital transformation, supply chain risk and resilience, sustainability and the circular economy, and the future of global supply chain design and management. Entries in the series are international in outlook, providing fresh and innovative approaches to pressing issues in logistics and supply chain management.

Priscilla Schelp · Heather Skipworth ·
Emel Aktas · Beate Vieth

Supply Chain Disruptions and Stock Prices

The Effects of Hurricane-Induced Disruptions on Company Stock Price

palgrave
macmillan

Priscilla Schelp
Cranfield School of Management
Cranfield, UK

Emel Aktas
School of Management
Cranfield University
Cranfield, UK

Heather Skipworth
Cranfield School of Management
Cranfield University
Cranfield, UK

Beate Vieth
Ludwig-Maximilians-Universität
München
Munich, Germany

Palgrave Studies in Logistics and Supply Chain Management
ISBN 978-3-031-68884-3 ISBN 978-3-031-68885-0 (eBook)
https://doi.org/10.1007/978-3-031-68885-0

This Palgrave Macmillan imprint is published by the registered company Springer Nature Switzerland AG
The registered company address is: Gewerbestrasse 11, 6330 Cham, Switzerland

Priscilla Schelp is dedicating this book to the great support of Heather, Emel, Beate & Thomas during her research!

Heather and Emel dedicate this book to all supply chain professionals around the world who work tirelessly to recover from disruptions.

Beate dedicates this book to Priscilla for her trust and Thomas for his great support.

Foreword

The increased globalisation of supply chains in recent decades has resulted in a profound and significant change in the risk profile of supply chains. Global trade results in multiple manufacturing locations connected by multiple modes of transport over land, sea and air resulting in multiple channels and routing to the final end customer. The complex network of modern supply chains is at times vulnerable to disruption but can also have an in-built resilience enabling businesses to rapidly reconfigure the network to cope with disruption.

There are numerous disruptions experienced by modern supply chains, from natural events to geopolitical events to general business incompetence and decision making resulting in lack of supply! Recognising that supply chain resilience requires organisation to prepare for disruptions, to respond to the disruption but importantly to recover from the disruption to enable to business the maintain its operations to sustain its economic viability is increasingly important. "Prepare, Respond and Recover" requires a proactive approach forcing an organisation to review processes, the supply chain network and infrastructure, the information systems used and importantly the people and organisation structures to embed supply chain resilience physically but also "culturally" within an organisation and across the extended supply network. Proactivity requires resources and investment to prepare for events that may occur rarely or occasionally. In a world where the executive board is often focused on shareholder value and their annual bonus, this investment may not at times be forthcoming!

But is there a business case for investing in supply chain resilience? Recent significant global disruptions have highlighted "costs" to businesses. Disruptions to the logistics flows through the Suez and Panama canals increase logistics costs of re-routing container vessels, the pandemic led to shortages and increased costs and inflation, geopolitical events resulting in energy price fluctuations which has resulted in further loss of consumer purchasing power globally, a toxic mix of both supply disruption and demand disruption are recognised to "cost" businesses dearly. All these events can be seen to have impacted global stock markets and reduced business confidence.

This book looks at the impact of a regularly occurring natural event, the hurricane, hurricanes have "seasons" they are not "random", they regularly occur and organisations can pro-actively prepare, have plans to respond and importantly recover. With these in place the evidence presented shows that any impact on customers and shareholders can be reduced. The learning has applicability to other supply chain disruptions so organisations who feel "immune" to hurricanes due to there geographical location can take principles and apply them to their current situation. All supply chains at times experience metaphorical "hurricanes" resulting in disruption.

Creating resilient supply chains is a passion of mine, the resilient supply chain ensures economic, social and environmental sustainability, protecting our profits, people and planet. Understanding how supply chain disruption can influence stock prices is important for all business leaders to recognise and act upon. This research provides thought provoking insights for both academics and practitioners alike, providing ideas on how to prepare, respond and recover thus contributing to our efforts to the creation of a more resilient and sustainable world.

Professor Richard Wilding OBE, is a multi award winning business educator and executive specialising in global supply chains. He is author and presenter of "Supply Chain Fundamentals: Risk and Resilience" a highly successful LinkedIn Learning Course.

Rugby, UK
March 2024

Professor Richard Wilding, OBE

Preface

Supply chain disruptions typically have a negative effect on stock prices. This effect is stronger if a catastrophe causes the disruption. While supply chains in the United States suffer from a wide range of supply chain disruptions induced by hurricanes, the impact of these disruptions on stock prices remains unexplored, even though the annual average hurricane damage in the US due to hurricanes is $54bn, of which $9bn affects commercial businesses.

This book provides a framework connecting disasters, supply chain disruptions, and firm performance, thereby bridging supply chain management and financial economics literature. The book presents evaluations of the effect of hurricane-induced supply chain disruptions for the first time. It identifies potential influencing factors and tests if and in which way these influence the effect of hurricanes on stock prices.

It discusses the effects of incident and hurricane announcements by comparing both. It uses the event study methodology, specifically Autoregressive Integrated Moving Average (ARIMA), in combination with an intervention model to evaluate the effect of hurricane announcements and incident announcements on the daily stock price time series of manufacturing firms.

Longer-term effects are evaluated, and the best-fitting functions are assessed. The research presented in this book accounts for autocorrelation, trend, seasonality, and drift patterns. Additionally, the effects of influencing factors such as impact type, impact extent, detailed damage, disruption size, sector and preventive closure are tested as a contribution to the existing literature.

This book provides guidelines to managers who need to make decisions on how to communicate supply chain disruptions to their customers and shareholders. The findings show that firms should communicate hurricane-induced disruptions in a transparent way, as this reduces shareholders' uncertainty, so the stock price reactions are less negative. For instance, providing details on actual damage leads to a less negative, and mostly positive, stock price reaction and providing information on preventative closures mainly prevents negative stock reaction.

Cranfield, UK — Priscilla Schelp
Cranfield, UK — Heather Skipworth
Cranfield, UK — Emel Aktas
Munich, Germany — Beate Vieth
November 2023

Contents

Acronyms

AIC	Akaike Information Criterion
ARIMA	Auto-Regressive Integrated Moving Average
CAR	Cumulative Abnormal Return
LRT	Likelihood Ratio Tests
NYSE	New York Stock Exchange
SCD	Supply Chain Disruption
SCM	Supply Chain Management
SCRM	Supply Chain Risk Management
SEC	Securities and Exchange Commission
UNDRR	United Nations Office for Disaster Risk Reduction

List of Figures

CHAPTER 1

Supply Chain Risk Management

Abstract This chapter establishes the foundational concepts of Supply Chain Risk Management (SCRM), focusing on risks arising from natural disasters. It clarifies the distinctions between risk and uncertainty, emphasising their critical roles in supply chain disruptions. The chapter explores both upside and downside risks, integrating perspectives from decision theory and finance, while addressing the debate between objective and subjective risk assessments. Positioned within the broader field of Supply Chain Management, this chapter traces the evolution of SCRM from firm-level concerns to a holistic, supply chain-wide approach. By providing a detailed typology of supply chain risks and disruptions, it offers essential insights for understanding the impact of disasters on firm performance, setting the stage for deeper exploration in subsequent chapters.

Keywords Supply Chain Risk Management · Natural Disasters · Risk Uncertainty · Supply Chain Disruptions · Risk Typology · Firm Performance · Objective Risk · Subjective Risk · Upside Risk · Downside Risk

This chapter sets the scene in terms of supply chain risk management with a focus on natural disasters. Supply Chain Risk Management (SCRM)

P. Schelp et al., *Supply Chain Disruptions and Stock Prices*, Palgrave Studies in Logistics and Supply Chain Management,
https://doi.org/10.1007/978-3-031-68885-0_1

is an essential aspect of modern business operations, especially in an era marked by increasing global connectivity and complexity. This chapter serves as the foundation for our exploration of SCRM, with a particular focus on risks stemming from natural disasters. We introduce fundamental concepts of supply chain management, risk, and uncertainty, providing clear definitions and insights. We also provide the required definitions and classifications around the three key concepts: disasters, supply chain disruptions, and firm performance.

1.1 Definitions of Supply Chain Management, Risk, and Uncertainty

In the realm of SCRM, it is crucial to establish a clear understanding of the key terms that underpin our discussions. Definitions provide the framework upon which our exploration is built, allowing us to navigate the multifaceted world of supply chains, risks, and uncertainties.

1.1.1 Risk Versus Uncertainty

Risk, as a concept, is multifaceted and manifests differently across various disciplines and research areas. Risk is exposure to a proposition of which one is uncertain, where exposure captures the personal interest in what transpires (Holton, 2004). Risk is about choice, which actions we take, depending on how free we are to choose between alternatives (Khan & Burnes, 2007). In Transaction Cost Economics, the initial assumption that transactors are risk-neutral has been extended to incorporate how attitudes toward (risk-seeking vs risk-averse) affect the relationship between asset specificity and governance cost (Chiles & McMackin, 1996). In supply chain management, the risk sources are categorised as environmental, industry, organisational, problem-specific, and decision-maker-related (Rao & Goldsby, 2009).

Within our context, risk refers to the likelihood of variance in expected outcomes, and it is quantifiable. In other words, risk can be measured in terms of the probability of occurrence and the impact it has, introducing variance from the expected outcome. This perspective aligns with the notion that risk is associated with known outcomes (Khan & Burnes, 2007; Lockamy III, 2014).

Conversely, uncertainty is fundamentally different from risk in that it cannot be quantified or measured, as the possible outcomes are unknown

(Knight, 1921). Uncertainty arises when the possible outcomes are unknown, leaving us without a clear basis for measurement. However, risk and uncertainty are interconnected. Risk can be seen as a form of uncertainty associated with a known outcome, indicating that there is no unknown risk (Yates & Stone, 1992). Therefore, can be seen as a key determinant of risk. In the context of supply chains, natural and man-made disasters are prime sources of uncertainties that can give rise to supply chain risks (Lockamy III, 2014; Tang, 2006). In line with the earlier definition by Holton (2004), a risk may be defined in the supply chain context as "exposure to a premise, the outcome of which is uncertain" (Rao & Goldsby, 2009, p. 100).

1.1.2 Upside Versus Downside Risk

The most widely known definition of risk is that an outcome is worse than expected—a so-called downside risk (Arrow, 1970). However, some research in decision theory and finance argues that risk is not just the downside but also the upside possibility, such as a higher performance than expected (Arrow, 1970; Kahneman & Tversky, 1979; Rao & Goldsby, 2009; Wagner & Bode, 2008). This implies that a risk can be viewed as a deviation from the expected outcome—in whatever direction. This discussion is also reflected in the supply chain risk research, which considers upside and downside risk and defines supply chain risk as a "variation in the distribution of possible supply chain outcomes, their likelihood, and their subjective value" (Jüttner et al., 2003, p. 200).

While some theories in decision-making and finance argue that risk encompasses both upside and downside possibilities, including the potential for higher-than-expected performance, most business researchers and supply chain experts tend to focus on downside risks as these are typically perceived as more threatening to organisations than upside risks. However, previous research showed that, after a natural disaster, some industrial sectors show upside risks as some firms might benefit from the crisis and experience higher demands. Both positive and negative reactions are possible, especially in the aftermath of events like natural disasters (Khan & Burnes, 2007). Thus, the risk is not limited to the downside possibility and includes the deviation/fluctuation from the expected outcome, thereby causing a lack of controllability (Wagner & Bode, 2008).

In the context of our research, we assess both downside and upside risk. We examine the effects of hurricanes and hurricane-related incidents on stock prices, recognising that some firms may experience negative stock price reactions due to expected damage, while others may see positive movements because they produce essential goods needed after such events (Chiles & McMackin, 1996; Khan & Burnes, 2007; Jüttner et al., 2003).

1.1.3 Objective Versus Subjective Risk

Whether risk is subjective or objective is an ongoing debate in the field of risk management theory (Khan & Burnes, 2007). Some researchers emphasise the subjective nature of risk, using terms like "perception" or "perceived" to denote a more subjective perspective (Cousins et al., 2004; Kraljic, 1983; Williamson, 1979). Another theory, underlying the subjectivity is the utility theory which states that customers make buying decisions based on the degree of utility or satisfaction they gain (Witt, 2016). Others employ terms such as "probability" to indicate a more objective view of supply chain risks (Harland et al., 2003; Khan & Burnes, 2007).

The discussion of risk as either objective or subjective does not seem to be broadly reflected in the academic supply chain risk literature (Khan & Burnes, 2007). In practice, many business executives prefer risk management approaches that combine both subjective and objective measures (Hendricks & Singhal, 2005a; Hood & Rothstein, 2001). This approach allows for flexibility in decision-making, enabling executives to consider various factors beyond quantitative analysis (Hendricks & Singhal, 2005a). Additionally, it acknowledges that risks can affect different stakeholders within a business in distinct ways.

While the debate between objective and subjective risk persists, it is essential to reflect on this discussion in the context of supply chain risk literature. Recognising the implications of this debate on how risks are perceived and managed is crucial. Our research aligns with a contingency view, acknowledging the validity of both objective and subjective perspectives on supply chain risks (Hendricks & Singhal, 2005a; Hood & Rothstein, 2001).

1.2 Positioning in the Supply Chain Management Research

Our research contributes significantly to the field of Supply Chain Management (SCM), specifically within the realm of Supply Chain Risk Management (SCRM). Supply chain risks are no longer confined to practical application but have garnered increasing academic interest in recent years. There is extensive SCM literature available on supply chain risks in general. The literature most relevant to this research is presented in the following subsections.

1.2.1 Supply Chains, Supply Chain Management and Supply Chain Risk Management

To understand SCRM fully, it is essential to grasp the broader concepts of supply chains and supply chain management. Supply chains represent interconnected networks of trading partners linked by the flow of materials, information, and finances (Fugate et al., 2006; Spekman & Davis, 2004). Effective supply chains maximise value for all participants and customers (Lockamy III, 2014). Supply Chain Management (SCM) takes a holistic approach to address business challenges by aligning global supply and demand while considering complexity and uncertainty (Lockamy III, 2014).

An increasing number of organisations are adopting SCM principles (Kopczak & Johnson, 2003) as supply chains are becoming increasingly global, complex, and dynamic, and thereby more exposed to external risks (Harland et al., 2003; Khan & Burnes, 2007; Jüttner, 2005; Wagner & Bode, 2008). Due to the increase in supply chain risk literature, there are some slightly varying definitions of SCRM available (Rao & Goldsby, 2009).

Most SCRM definitions state that "SCRM is an extension of the within-firm risk management ideology" (Rao & Goldsby, 2009, p. 101). SCRM extends the principles of risk management beyond individual firms and emphasises a coordinated approach involving all supply chain members to reduce overall supply chain vulnerability (Christopher et al., 2002). Another view is to ensure profitability and continuity as the purpose of SCRM (Tang, 2006). Despite varying definitions, there is consensus among supply chain researchers that SCRM's primary purpose is to enhance resilience at the holistic supply chain level, moving beyond the traditional focus on individual firm risk management (Rao & Goldsby, 2009). This view is adopted for this research.

1.2.2 Evolution of Supply Chain Risk Management

The evolution of research in supply chain management has seen a significant shift in focus over time. Initially, academic interest in risk management within the supply chain context was limited, with some early work on procurement-related risks dating back to the 1960s (Eisenhardt, 1989; Hallikas et al., 2004; Harland et al., 2003; Kraljic, 1983; Zsidisin et al., 2000). However, a notable transformation occurred in the past 15 years, marked by a transition from managing risks within the confines of institutions to adopting a more comprehensive and holistic perspective on supply chain risks (Cousins et al., 2004; Harland et al., 2003; Khan & Burnes, 2007; Lewis, 2003; Peck, 2006; Wieland & Wallenburg, 2012).

One driving factor behind this change in perspective is the growing complexity, dynamism, and globalisation of supply chains. As supply chains have expanded globally, they have become more susceptible to external risks, including political, economic events, and natural disasters (Harland et al., 2003; Khan & Burnes, 2007; Wagner & Bode, 2008). This heightened exposure to a wide range of risks prompted researchers to explore the relationship between risk and supply chain management more deeply.

Many of these researchers built upon earlier studies conducted in the 1960s that examined risks in procurement. Their investigations aimed to establish a connection between risk and supply chain management, with an emphasis on understanding how natural disasters, such as hurricanes, impact supply chains and subsequently affect firm performance (Altay & Ramirez, 2010; Aula, 2010; Khan & Burnes, 2007). This research also sought to identify and assess these supply chain risks, leading to the development of strategies for SCRM aimed at reducing the adverse effects of such risks.

Our research integrates elements of risk management theory and financial performance analysis, drawing from the extensive body of literature in financial economics. Financial economics literature places a strong emphasis on quantitative measurements and detailed modelling, which is particularly relevant when analysing the financial impact of events (Dryden, 1969). Event studies, for instance, play a vital role in this context (Flouris & Walker, 2007; Kannan et al., 2007).

In summary, this research effort consolidates insights from both supply chain management and financial economics literature to establish connections among three central concepts: disasters, supply chain disruptions (SCDs), and firm performance (Fig. 1.1). The management perspective is represented by the yellow area on the left, while the financial economics literature is depicted in the red area on the right. The overlapping circles symbolise the interplay among these three key concepts, reflecting their interconnected nature. The research question is situated within this overlap, as it seeks to explore the relationships and effects within this dynamic framework.

SCRM has evolved over the years, transitioning from a narrow focus on risk identification and mitigation within individual organisations to a broader perspective encompassing the entire supply chain. Early SCRM efforts primarily involved the assessment of risks associated with individual suppliers or specific supply chain nodes.

However, this limited approach failed to address the interdependencies and ripple effects that risks could have across the entire supply chain. As a response to various high-profile disruptions and disasters, researchers

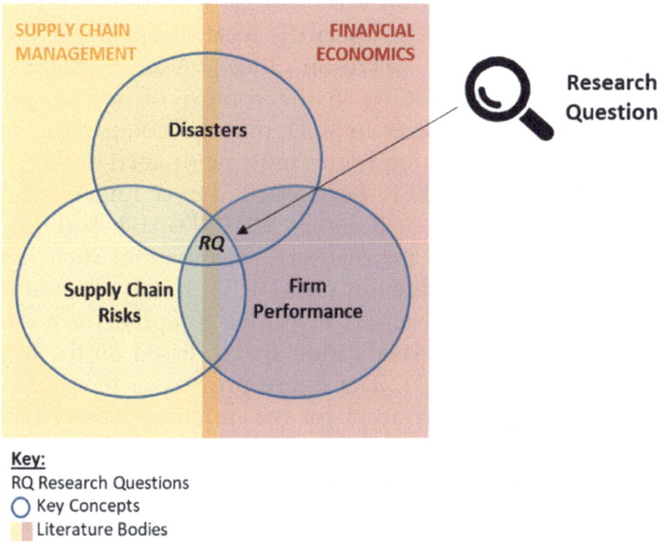

Fig. 1.1 Key concepts and literature bodies (*Source* Authors)

and practitioners began advocating for a more comprehensive approach to SCRM. This approach emphasises collaboration among supply chain partners and the development of strategies that enhance supply chain resilience in the face of various risks (Tang, 2006; Chopra & Sodhi, 2004; Sheffi & Rice Jr, 2005).

1.3 The Significance of Disasters in Supply Chain Risk Management

Disasters such as man-made and natural disasters can have catastrophic effects on supply chains. These events are particularly significant due to their ability to disrupt entire regions, resulting in damage to infrastructure, transportation, and communication systems. The consequences of such disruptions can be felt far beyond the immediate disaster area, affecting supply chains on a global scale.

1.3.1 Disasters

Natural disasters have the potential to inflict severe disruptions within supply chains. These disruptions can manifest as damage to the production sites of upstream suppliers, affect the focal company itself, or result in transportation disturbances (Wilson, 2007). A key factor in causing a supply chain disruption (SCD) in the context of natural disasters is geographic proximity. To trigger an SCD, the focal company, its upstream suppliers, or their transportation routes must be situated in the vicinity of the natural disaster (Kaplanski & Levy, 2010; Tan & Enderwick, 2006).

Various researchers (Altay & Ramirez, 2010; Dada & Jagboro, 2007), as well as governmental and international organisations such as the UN Office for Disaster Risk Reduction (UNDRR), have proposed different classifications for natural disasters. To ensure a comprehensive categorisation, this research adopts a classification system based on the underlying natural phenomena (Fig. 1.2). The figure provides a breakdown structure of the natural disaster concept for the different disaster types. This classification encompasses four primary groups (Dada & Jagboro, 2007):

Climatological events: This category includes occurrences like heatwaves, freezes, wildfires, and droughts.

Hydrological events: Encompassing flash floods, river floods, storm surges, and mass movements (landslides).

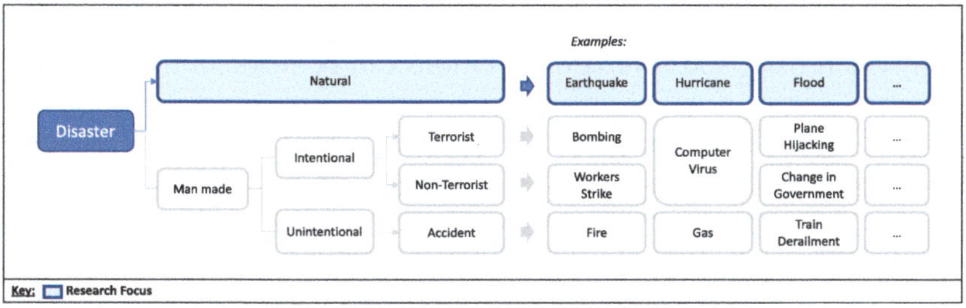

Fig. 1.2 Classification of natural disasters (Adapted from Dada & Jagboro, 2007)

Meteorological events: The most diverse category, including tropical storms, winter storms, severe weather, hailstorms, tornadoes, local storms, hurricanes, and blizzards.

Geophysical events: These events, such as earthquakes and volcanic eruptions, are driven by tectonic movements.

In addition to these natural disasters, diseases and epidemics are considered within the natural disaster category, even though they represent special cases. Examples include viruses like SARS and the Coronavirus (Flouris & Walker, 2007; Vasigh & Fleming, 2005; Tan & Enderwick, 2006). Diseases can also be viewed as man-made events if used as bio-weapons.

For the purposes of this thesis, the focus is specifically on hurricanes, which fall under the meteorological disasters category. This choice is supported by descriptive analysis, revealing that 82% of disaster incidents involving firms listed on the New York Stock Exchange (NYSE) are attributed to hurricanes.

1.3.2 A Typology of Supply Chain Risks

In the realm of supply chain management, numerous scholarly works have endeavoured to identify and delineate various types of supply chain risks. These categorisations typically assign uncertainties or "supply chain risk sources" to specific "risk events" (Jüttner, 2005; Lockamy III, 2014; Spekman & Davis, 2004; Zsidisin & Wagner, 2010). This terminology, involving risk sources and events, aligns with the broader academic literature on risk management (Ritchie & Marshall, 1993).

There is no universally accepted classification or categorisation for supply chain risks, and several observations can be made in this regard:

1. **Classification Approach:** The manner in which risks are classified hinges on the perspective taken. Some researchers classify risks based on their sources, while others categorise them by the nature of the risk event itself (Jüttner, 2005; Lockamy III, 2014; Zsidisin & Wagner, 2010). While many supply chain researchers categorise supply chain risk events by their sources, a smaller number opt for classifying by the risk event, and no typology was identified to be exclusively based on risk impact (Spekman & Davis, 2004).
2. **Scope of Focus:** In the realm of supply chain risk research, there is a disparity in focus. Some researchers concentrate solely on the risk event known as supply chain disruption (SCD), while others take a broader perspective, considering supply chain risks in a general sense (Craighead et al., 2007; Jüttner et al., 2003; Wieland & Wallenburg, 2012).
3. **Terminology and Grouping:** The terminology employed and the way researchers group risk sources exhibit variability (Craighead et al. 2007; Rao & Goldsby 2009; Wieland & Wallenburg 2012). There is no standardised academic consensus on a particular terminology and grouping of risks.

Many supply chain researchers tend to focus on risks that culminate in supply chain disruptions (SCDs). This emphasises the significance of SCDs within the supply chain risk literature (Craighead et al., 2007; Jüttner et al., 2003; Wieland & Wallenburg, 2012). However, these typologies can be viewed as SCD typologies rather than comprehensive supply chain risk typologies, as they often exclude risks such as Corporate Social Responsibility (CSR) risks.

To address these complexities, a three-category typology is employed here to classify SCD sources, encompassing **Operational Risks** (within the firm), **Network Risks** (outside the firm but within the supply chain), and **External/Environmental Risks** (outside the supply chain). Nevertheless, the chosen typology aligns with the approach undertaken by Rao and Goldsby (2009), as it aligns with the broader risk management literature (Ritchie & Marshall, 1993). Rao and Goldsby (2009) categorise risk sources into five primary categories: environmental factors, industry factors, organisational factors, problem-specific factors, and decision-maker-related factors. Among these, environmental factors, industry factors, and organisational factors are regarded as framework factors that represent the circumstances and environment within which an organisation operates.

Supply chain risks can exert a substantial influence on a company's overall performance. Research within the realms of Supply Chain and Financial Economics has established a link between two specific categories of supply chain risk events and their significant impact on firm performance. These categories are Corporate Social Responsibility (CSR) risks (Giannakis & Papadopoulos, 2016; Humphrey et al., 2016; Nuryaman, 2013; Wang & Berens, 2015) and supply chain disruption risks (Blackhurst et al., 2005; Chopra & Sodhi, 2004; Hendricks & Singhal, 2005a, 2005b).

This research endeavour is specifically directed towards the exploration of supply chain disruptions (SCDs), and there are several compelling reasons for this choice:

Firstly, externally induced SCDs stand as a significant concern for organisations due to their inherently unpredictable and uncontrollable nature (Barnett & Hoffman, 2008; Fauchart & Cowan, 2014; Jüttner, 2005; Petersen & Lemke, 2015).

Secondly, the incidence of SCDs is on the rise, driven by factors such as diseases, terrorist attacks, and natural disasters (Jüttner, 2005; Khan & Burnes, 2007).

Thirdly, valuable data regarding the causes of external SCDs are readily available through internet sources and media channels, including early warnings and historical information pertaining to natural calamities like tsunamis.

Lastly, there is a relative scarcity of research that focuses comprehensively on assessing the impact of SCDs within the context of supply chain risks.

To provide a visual representation, a basic typology for supply chain risks is presented in Fig. 1.3.

1.3.3 Supply Chain Disruptions as Supply Chain Risks

Supply chain disruptions (SCDs) represent a specific category of supply chain risk, and within the literature, these risks are subject to various classification methods. For instance, they can be categorised based on

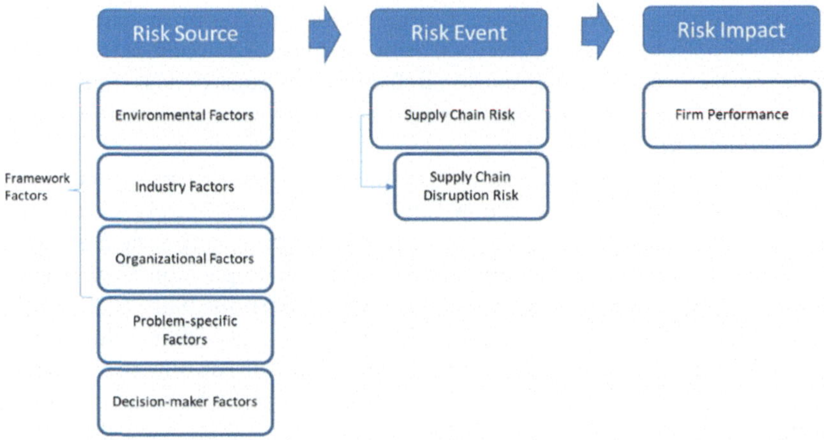

Fig. 1.3 Supply chain risk typology (Based on Rao & Goldsby 2009)

their source, underlying causes, primary locations of occurrence, disruption of flow, or duration. Among these classification approaches, the most prevalent ones for SCDs are rooted in the source and cause of disruption (Filbeck et al., 2016; Hendricks & Singhal, 2003, 2005a, 2005b; Hendricks et al., 2009; Wagner & Neshat, 2012).

Some researchers opt to employ multiple classifications or combinations thereof, such as considering both the source and cause. This multifaceted approach allows for diverse perspectives on SCDs (Hendricks & Singhal, 2005a, 2005b). In certain instances, researchers interchangeably use the terms "cause" and "source" (Filbeck et al., 2016; Hendricks & Singhal, 2008; Wagner & Neshat, 2012).

Concerning SCDs, the term "risk cause" appears to be frequently utilised, thus prompting an extension of the supply chain risk typology by introducing this dimension (Fig. 1.4).

Fig. 1.4 Characteristics of supply chain disruption

In this book, the assessment of SCDs encompasses four dimensions: risk source, risk cause, risk event, and risk impact (Stecke & Kumar, 2009). The examination of SCDs in this work incorporates an evaluation of these four dimensions, which can be effectively identified and assessed by posing specific and dedicated questions.

Risk Source

The term "source" in the context of supply chain disruptions (SCDs) refers to the classification of responsibility for these disruptions (Hendricks & Singhal, 2003; Hendricks et al., 2009; Macdonald & Corsi, 2013) as depicted in Fig. 1.4. This dimension is also referred to as "responsibility", "primary source", and "location" (Filbeck et al., 2016; Hendricks & Singhal, 2005a, 2005b, 2008; Hendricks et al., 2009; Kumar et al., 2015; Macdonald & Corsi, 2013; Thun & Hoenig, 2011; Wagner & Neshat, 2012).

The risk source can be categorised as either internal or external to the supply chain, as well as environmental (Kumar et al., 2015; Thun & Hoenig, 2011). Internal may be defined as within the company (Hendricks & Singhal, 2008) or within the specific supply chain under evaluation (Thun & Hoenig, 2011) or both (Kumar et al., 2015). When discussing within the supply chain, it may also involve the examination of supply chain structure (Wagner & Neshat, 2012). In this context, "internal" is defined as within the supply chain, encompassing all supply chain members, such as suppliers, the focal company itself, retailers, and customers (Kumar et al., 2015; Wagner & Neshat, 2012). The term "company-internal" is employed to denote risks originating within the focal company itself (Hendricks & Singhal, 2003; Hendricks et al., 2009; Thun & Hoenig, 2011).

On the other hand, external SCDs are those caused by sources outside of the supply chain (Christopher & Peck, 2004) and are often associated with environmental causes that are challenging to influence (Kumar et al., 2015; Thun & Hoenig, 2011). This category can be further subdivided considering factors such as government, regulatory bodies, and natural occurrences as sources of responsibility (Hendricks & Singhal, 2005a, 2005b, 2008). SCDs may not always be attributed to a single source (Hendricks & Singhal, 2005a, 2005b; Kumar et al., 2015). For instance, hurricanes, like many other disasters, are typically classified as external events (Kleindorfer & Saad, 2005).

Risk Cause

The term "risk cause", or sometimes referred to as "risk reason", pertains to identifying the underlying factors or "what" led to the occurrence of SCDs. SCDs can be attributed to various risk causes, both originating within and outside the supply chain (Zsidisin & Wagner, 2010). There exist several classification methods for these causes (Filbeck et al., 2016; Hendricks & Singhal, 2003, 2005a, 2005b; Hendricks et al., 2009).

In the context of supply chain risks, categorisation by cause is commonly employed (Rao & Goldsby, 2009), aligning with the broader principles of risk management literature (Ritchie & Marshall, 1993). Supply chain risks can be broadly classified into five principal categories: environmental, industrial, organisational, problem-specific, and decision-making factors. Environmental causes, including natural uncertainties, play a significant role in triggering major SCDs (Stecke & Kumar, 2009). Hurricanes, for example, are categorised as a natural uncertainty within this classification.

Risk Event

The term "risk event", often referred to as "supply chain disruption", is characterised as a situation of supply and demand misalignment (Hendricks & Singhal, 2005a). This misalignment can manifest as a disruption in the flow of goods, information, or financial resources (Akintoye & MacLeod, 1997; Jüttner et al., 2003; Reason, 1990; Shrivastava et al., 2020; Swierczek, 2016).

Such disruptions have the potential to occur at various points within the supply chain. These disruptions may manifest upstream within the supply chain, involving suppliers, occur within the focal company itself, or take place downstream in the supply chain at customer-related junctures (Kumar et al., 2015). Figure 1.5 shows the disruption as a risk event.

In this particular study, the focus is directed towards supply chain disruptions (SCDs) occurring upstream within the supply chain or within the focal company itself. This choice is made due to the heightened level of threat posed by disruptions in these locations (Altay and Ramirez, 2010; Giunipero & Aly Eltantawy, 2004).

Risk Impact

Supply chain disruptions have exerted notable and tangible adverse effects, both directly and indirectly, on aspects such as corporate reputation, operational efficiency, operating performance, and stock price

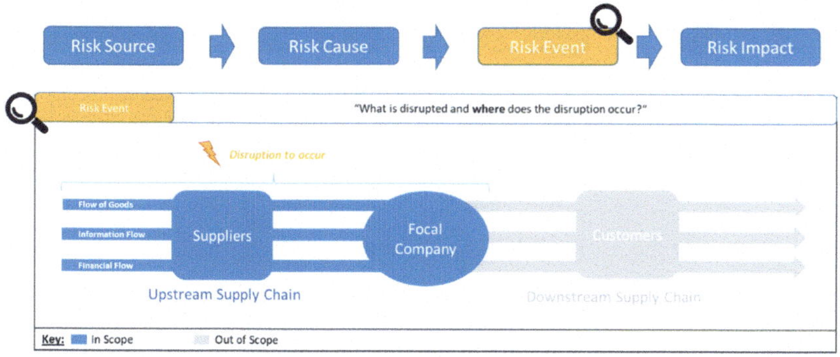

Fig. 1.5 Schematic of supply chain disruption event

performance (Altay & Ramirez, 2010; Aula, 2010; Khan & Burnes, 2007; Zsidisin & Wagner, 2010). While the negative financial repercussions of supply chain disruptions are evident, the severity of these impacts can vary considerably (Hendricks & Singhal, 2005a; Zsidisin et al., 2016).

Furthermore, there exists a well-established connection between Supply Chain Management (SCM) practices and a firm's financial performance, substantiating the critical importance of effective SCM and thereby underscoring the significance of this subject (Ellinger et al., 2011; Johnson & Templar, 2011; Shi & Yu, 2013).

Figure 1.6 provides a concise summary of the four distinct dimensions within the supply chain context: risk source, risk cause, risk event, and risk impact. The delineation of these dimensions is indicated through shading, facilitating a comprehensive overview of the focus of this book.

1.3.4 Firm Performance

Various terms, such as "business performance" (Neely, 1998) or "organisational performance", are used interchangeably to describe what we commonly refer to as "firm performance". Only what is measured can be effectively managed, underscoring the critical importance of measuring organisational performance (Neely, 1998). However, while having a robust performance measurement system is crucial, its real value lies in the selection and execution of effective actions. This implies that the means to control firm performance are of paramount importance. Nevertheless, this approach can sometimes lead to gaming behaviour, where

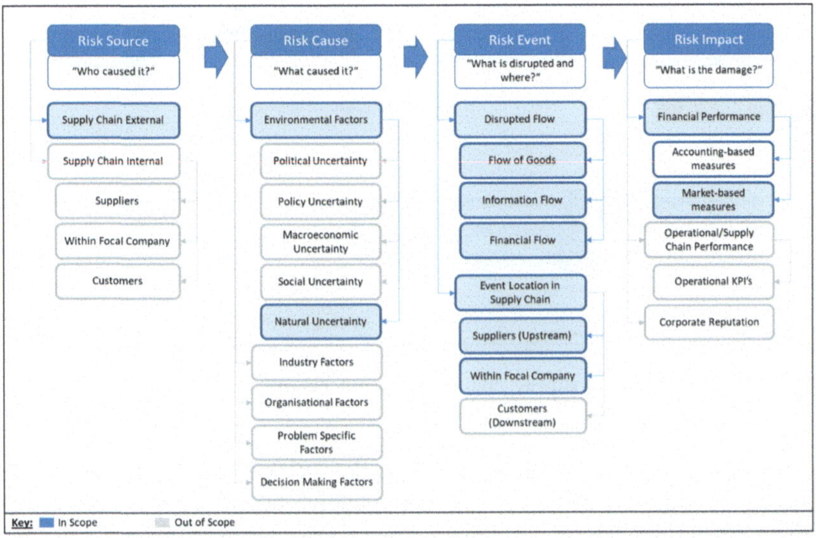

Fig. 1.6 Supply chain disruption: Overview of definition and scoping as indicated by shading

manipulating performance measures may have a similar or even better impact on the measured firm's performance compared to managing the actual performance itself. Consequently, alternative performance measurement frameworks and tools have been developed, including the balanced scorecard, activity-based costing, shareholder value analysis, market value analysis, and throughput accounting (Neely, 1998).

Firm financial performance can be assessed using accounting ratios to determine book value or market-based measures that gauge market or shareholder value (Filbeck et al., 2016; Shi & Yu, 2013). Book value is calculated as the shareholder's equity, obtained by subtracting the liabilities from the organisation's assets as presented in the balance sheet (Penman, 2013). Notably, market/shareholder value is often distinct from book value, exemplified by some of the world's largest companies like Coca-Cola (Neely, 1998). Investors evaluate not only the tangible assets but also intangible assets, such as patents, and respond to new information, resulting in disparities between book value and market/shareholder value (Filbeck et al., 2016; Marcus & Goodman, 1989; Neely, 1998). An equity market's response depends on various factors, including prices, trading volume, location, spreads, and volatility (Brooks et al., 2003; Chen et al., 2015), leading to market-based financial measures such as Tobin's Q, the Sharpe Ratio, and abnormal stock returns (Shi & Yu, 2013).

In contrast, supply chain or operational performance is typically assessed using operational key performance indicators (KPIs) such as "Orders Delivered in Full" and "Order Fill Rate" (Ainapur et al., 2011). Corporate reputation, while influential on customer and stakeholder perception, is challenging to quantify (Humphrey et al., 2016; Khan & Burnes, 2007; Suh & Amine, 2007). However, several frameworks exist in the strategic management and marketing literature to provide some guidance (Alsop, 2004; Dowling, 2001; Fombrun, 1996; Jackson, 2004; Feldman et al., 2014; Suh & Amine, 2007; Vidaver-Cohen & Brønn, 2015).

Firm performance can be assessed through various parameters and methods, including financial performance, operational/supply chain performance, and corporate reputation (as illustrated in Fig. 1.7). Research papers often tend to focus on one specific measure of firm performance. Notably, when measuring the impact of disasters and external/accident-caused supply chain disruptions, evaluating market-based measures appears to be a common approach. The availability of data plays a crucial role in research, and stock price data, being publicly accessible with frequent data points (daily), is often preferred. In contrast, many other firm performance data, such as operational KPIs, may not be publicly available, or financial records may be reported on a quarterly basis, making it more challenging to evaluate the effect of events such as disasters. This book analyses stock prices (not stock price returns) as the applied model accounts for various factors, including autocorrelation, non-stationarity, trends, seasonal and cyclic changes, as well as drifts, thus yielding more accurate results.

Stock price data, being time series data, lend themselves well to analysis using an autoregressive integrated moving average (ARIMA) model (which will be discussed in more detail in Chapter 2). In conjunction with ARIMA, events such as the announcement of a hurricane or the occurrence of a hurricane incident can be defined as transfer functions. In this context, the primary focus will be on understanding pulse, step, and transitory changes within the time series data (Box & Tiao, 1975).

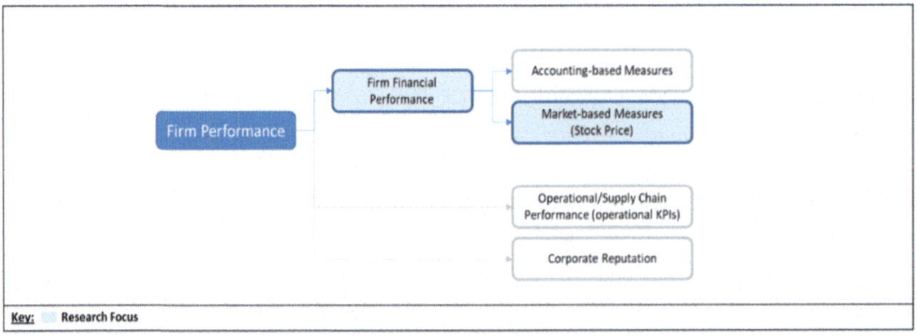

Fig. 1.7 Classification of firm performance

This chapter summarised the key concepts around risk management as well as supply chain risk management and provided the relevant definitions and classifications as a basis for this research.

References

Ainapur, B., Singh, R. K., Vittal, P. (2011). Strategic study on enhancement of supply chain performance. *International Journal of Business Insights & Transformation, 5*(1)

Akintoye, A. S., & MacLeod, M. J. (1997). Risk analysis and management in construction. *International Journal of Project Management, 15*(1), 31–38.

Alsop, R. J. (2004). Corporate reputation: Anything but superficial-the deep but fragile nature of corporate reputation. *Journal of Business Strategy, 25*(6), 21–29.

Altay, N., & Ramirez, A. (2010). Impact of disasters on firms in different sectors: Implications for supply chains. *Journal of Supply Chain Management, 46*(4), 59–80.

Arrow, K. J. (1970). *Essays in the theory of risk-bearing*. North-Holland.

Aula, P. (2010). Social media, reputation risk and ambient publicity management. *Strategy & Leadership, 38*(6), 43–49.

Barnett, M. L., & Hoffman, A. J. (2008). Beyond corporate reputation: Managing reputational interdependence. *Corporate Reputation Review, 11*, 1–9.

Blackhurst, J., Craighead, C. W., Elkins, D., & Handfield, R. B. (2005). An empirically derived agenda of critical research issues for managing supply-chain disruptions. *International Journal of Production Research, 43*(19), 4067–4081.

Box, G. E., & Tiao, G. C. (1975). Intervention analysis with applications to economic and environmental problems. *Journal of the American Statistical Association, 70*(349), 70–79.

Brooks, R. M., Patel, A., & Su, T. (2003). How the equity market responds to unanticipated events. *The Journal of Business, 76*(1), 109–133.

Chen, L. M., Liu, Y. E., & Yang, S. J. S. (2015). Robust supply chain strategies for recovering from unanticipated disasters. *Transportation Research Part E: Logistics and Transportation Review, 77*, 198–214.

Chiles, T. H., & McMackin, J. F. (1996). Integrating variable risk preferences, trust, and transaction cost economics. *Academy of Management Review, 21*(1), 73–99.

Chopra, S., & Sodhi, M. S. (2004). Managing risk to avoid supply-chain breakdown. *MIT Sloan Management Review, 46*(1), 53–61.

Christopher, M., & Peck, H. (2004). Building the resilient supply chain. *International Journal of Logistics Management, 15*(2), 1–14.

Christopher, M., McKinnon, A., Sharp, J., Wilding, R., Peck, H., Chapman, P., Juttner, U., & Bolumole, Y. (2002). *Supply chain vulnerability*. Cranfield University.

Cousins, P., Lamming, R., & Bowen, F. (2004). The role of risk in environment-related initiatives. *International Journal of Operations and Production Management, 24*(6), 554–565.

Craighead, C. W., Blackhurst, J., Rungtusanatham, M. J., & Handfield, R. B. (2007). The severity of supply chain disruptions: Design characteristics and mitigation capabilities. *Decision Sciences, 38*(1), 131–156.

Dada, J. O., & Jagboro, G. (2007). An evaluation of the impact of risk on project cost overrun in the Nigerian construction industry. *Journal of Financial Management of Property and Construction, 12*(1), 37–44.

Dowling, G. (2001). *Creating corporate reputations: Identity, image, and performance*. Oxford University Press.

Dryden, M. M. (1969). Share price movements: A Markovian approach. *The Journal of Finance, 24*(1), 49–60.

Eisenhardt, K. M. (1989). Building theories from case study research. *Academy of Management Review, 14*(4), 532–550.

Ellinger, A. E., Natarajarathinam, M., Adams, F. G., Gray, J. B., Hofman, D., & O'Marah, K. (2011). Supply chain management competency and firm financial success. *Journal of Business Logistics, 32*(3), 214–226.

Fauchart, E., & Cowan, R. (2014). Weak links and the management of reputational interdependencies. *Strategic Management Journal, 35*(4), 532–549.

Feldman, P. M., Bahamonde, R. A., & Velasquez Bellido, I. (2014). A new approach for measuring corporate reputation. *Revista de Administraçao de Empresas, 54*, 53–66.

Filbeck, G., Kumar, S., Liu, J., & Zhao, X. (2016). Supply chain finance and financial contagion from disruptions-evidence from the automobile industry. *International Journal of Physical Distribution & Logistics Management 46*(4)

Flouris, T., & Walker, T. (2007). Financial comparisons across different business models in the Canadian airline industry. *Journal of Air Transportation, 12*(1), 3–20.

Fombrun, C. J. (1996). *Reputation: Realizing value from the corporate image*. Harvard Business School Press.

Fugate, B., Sahin, F., & Mentzer, J. T. (2006). Supply chain management coordination mechanisms. *Journal of Business Logistics, 27*(2), 129–161.

Giannakis, M., & Papadopoulos, T. (2016). Supply chain sustainability: A risk management approach. *International Journal of Production Economics, 171*, 455–470.

Giunipero, L. C., & Aly Eltantawy, R. (2004). Securing the upstream supply chain: A risk management approach. *International Journal of Physical Distribution & Logistics Management, 34*(9), 698–713.

Hallikas, J., Karvonen, I., Pulkkinen, U., Virolainen, V. M., & Tuominen, M. (2004). Risk management processes in supplier networks. *International Journal of Production Economics, 90*(1), 47–58.

Harland, C., Brenchley, R., & Walker, H. (2003). Risk in supply networks. *Journal of Purchasing and Supply Management, 9*(2), 51–62.

Hendricks, K. B., & Singhal, V. R. (2003). The effect of supply chain glitches on shareholder wealth. *Journal of Operations Management, 21*(5), 501–522.

Hendricks, K. B., & Singhal, V. R. (2005a). Association between supply chain glitches and operating performance. *Management Science, 51*(5), 695–711.

Hendricks, K. B., & Singhal, V. R. (2005b). An empirical analysis of the effect of supply chain disruptions on long-run stock price performance and equity risk of the firm. *Production and Operations Management, 14*(1), 35–52.

Hendricks, K. B., & Singhal, V. R. (2008). The effect of supply chain disruptions on shareholder value. *Total Quality Management, 19*(7–8), 777–791.

Hendricks, K. B., Singhal, V. R., & Zhang, R. (2009). The effect of operational slack, diversification, and vertical relatedness on the stock market reaction to supply chain disruptions. *Journal of Operations Management, 27*(3), 233–246.

Holton, G. A. (2004). Defining risk. *Financial Analysts Journal, 60*(6), 19–25. https://doi.org/10.2469/faj.v60.n6.2669

Hood, C., & Rothstein, H. (2001). Risk regulation under pressure: Problem solving or blame shifting? *Administration & Society, 33*(1), 21–53.

Humphrey, P., Carter, D. A., & Simkins, B. (2016). The market's reaction to unexpected, catastrophic events: The case of oil and gas stock returns and the gulf oil spill. *The Journal of Risk Finance, 17*(1), 2–25.

Jackson, K. T. (2004). *Building reputational capital: Strategies for integrity and fair play that improve the bottom line*. Oxford University Press.

Johnson, M., & Templar, S. (2011). The relationships between supply chain and firm performance: The development and testing of a unified proxy. *International Journal of Physical Distribution & Logistics Management, 41*(2), 88–103.

Jüttner, U. (2005). Supply chain risk management: Understanding the business requirements from a practitioner perspective. *The International Journal of Logistics Management, 16*(1), 120–141.

Jüttner, U., Peck, H., & Christopher, M. (2003). Supply chain risk management: Outlining an agenda for future research. *International Journal of Logistics Research and Applications, 6*(4), 197–21. https://doi.org/10.1080/13675560310001627016

Kahneman, D., & Tversky, A. (1979). Prospect theory: An analysis of decision under risk. *Econometrica, 47*(2): 263–291. http://www.jstor.org/stable/1914185

Kannan, K., Rees, J., & Sridhar, S. (2007). Market reactions to information security breach announcements: An empirical analysis. *International Journal of Electronic Commerce, 12*(1), 69–91.

Kaplanski, G., & Levy, H. (2010). Sentiment and stock prices: The case of aviation disasters. *Journal of Financial Economics, 95*(2), 174–201.

Khan, O., & Burnes, B. (2007). Risk and supply chain management: Creating a research agenda. *The International Journal of Logistics Management, 18*(2), 197–216.

Kleindorfer, P. R., & Saad, G. H. (2005). Managing disruption risks in supply chains. *Production and Operations Management, 14*(1), 53–68.

Knight, F. H. (1921). *Risk, uncertainty and profit*. Houghton Mifflin.

Kopczak, L. R., & Johnson, M. E. (2003). The supply-chain management effect. *MIT Sloan Management Review, 44*(3), 27–34.

Kraljic, P. (1983). Purchasing must become supply chain management. *Harvard Business Review, 61*(5), 109–117.

Kumar, S., Liu, J., & Scutella, J. (2015). The impact of supply chain disruptions on stockholder wealth in India. *International Journal of Physical Distribution & Logistics Management, 45*(9/10), 938–958.

Lewis, M. A. (2003). Cause, consequence and control: Towards a theoretical and practical model of operational risk. *Journal of Operations Management, 21*(2), 205–224.

Lockamy, A., III. (2014). Assessing disaster risks in supply chains. *Industrial Management & Data Systems, 114*(5), 755–777.

Macdonald, J. R., & Corsi, T. M. (2013). Supply chain disruption management: Severe events, recovery, and performance. *Journal of Business Logistics, 34*(4), 270–288.

Marcus, A. A., & Goodman, R. (1989). Corporate adjustments to catastrophe: A study of investor reaction to Bhopal. *Industrial Crisis Quarterly, 3*(3), 213–234.

Neely, A. (1998). Measuring Business Performance. *The Economist.*

Nuryaman, C. (2013). The effect of corporate social responsibility activities on profitability and stock prices (studies on the companies listed on Indonesia stock exchange). *Journal of Global Management, 6*(1), 113–124.

Peck, H. (2006). Reconciling supply chain vulnerability, risk and supply chain management. *International Journal of Logistics: Research and Applications, 9*(2), 127–142.

Penman, S. H. (2013). *Financial statement analysis and security valuation* (2nd ed.). McGraw-Hill.

Petersen, H. L., & Lemke, F. (2015). Mitigating reputational risks in supply chains. *Supply Chain Management: An International Journal, 20*(5), 495–510.

Rao, S., & Goldsby, T. J. (2009). Supply chain risks: A review and typology. *The International Journal of Logistics Management, 20*(1), 97–123.

Reason, J. (1990). *Human error*. Cambridge University Press.

Ritchie, B., & Marshall, D. (1993). *Business risk management*. Chapman & Hall.

Sheffi, Y., & Rice, J. B., Jr. (2005). A supply chain view of the resilient enterprise. *MIT Sloan Management Review, 47*(1), 41–48.

Shi, M., & Yu, W. (2013). Supply chain management and financial performance: Literature review and future directions. *International Journal of Operations & Production Management, 33*(10), 1283–1317.

Shrivastava, P., Mitroff, I. I., Miller, D., & Miglani, A. (2020). Understanding industrial crises. In G. Mars & D. T. H. Weir (Ed.), *Risk management* (pp. 181–200). Routledge.

Spekman, R. E., & Davis, E. W. (2004). Risky business: Expanding the discussion on risk and the extended enterprise. *International Journal of Physical Distribution & Logistics Management, 34*(5), 414–433.

Stecke, K. E., & Kumar, S. (2009). Sources of supply chain disruptions, factors that breed vulnerability, and mitigating strategies. *Journal of Marketing Channels, 16*(3), 193–226.

Suh, T., & Amine, L. S. (2007). Defining and managing reputational capital in global markets. *Journal of Marketing Theory and Practice, 15*(3), 205–217.

Swierczek, A. (2016). The "snowball effect" in the transmission of disruptions in supply chains: The role of intensity and span of integration. *The International Journal of Logistics Management, 27*(3), 1002–1038.

Tan, W. J., & Enderwick, P. (2006). Managing threats in the global era: The impact and response to SARS. *Thunderbird International Business Review, 48*(4), 515–536.

Tang, C. S. (2006). Robust strategies for mitigating supply chain disruptions. *International Journal of Logistics: Research and Applications, 9*(1), 33–45.
Thun, J. H., & Hoenig, D. (2011). An empirical analysis of supply chain risk management in the German automotive industry. *International Journal of Production Economics, 131*(1), 242–249.
Vasigh, B., & Fleming, K. (2005). A total factor productivity based structure for tactical cluster assessment: Empirical investigation in the airline industry. *Journal of Air Transportation, 10*(1), 3–19.
Vidaver-Cohen, D., & Brønn, P. S. (2015). Reputation, responsibility, and stakeholder support in Scandinavian firms: A comparative analysis. *Journal of Business Ethics, 127*, 49–64.
Wagner, S. M., & Bode, C. (2008). An empirical examination of supply chain performance along several dimensions of risk. *Journal of Business Logistics, 29*(1), 307–325.
Wagner, S. M., & Neshat, N. (2012). A comparison of supply chain vulnerability indices for different categories of firms. *International Journal of Production Research, 50*(11), 2877–2891.
Wang, Y., & Berens, G. (2015). The impact of four types of corporate social performance on reputation and financial performance. *Journal of Business Ethics, 131*, 337–359.
Wieland, A., & Wallenburg, C. M. (2012). Dealing with supply chain risks: Linking risk management practices and strategies to performance. *International Journal of Physical Distribution & Logistics Management, 42*(10), 887–905.
Williamson, O. E. (1979). Transaction-cost economics: The governance of contractual relations. *The Journal of Law and Economics, 22*(2), 233–261.
Wilson, M. C. (2007). The impact of transportation disruptions on supply chain performance. *Transportation Research Part E: Logistics and Transportation Review, 43*(4), 295–320.
Witt, U. (2016). The transformations of utility theory: A behavioral perspective. *Journal of Bioeconomics, 18*, 211–228.
Yates, J. F., & Stone, E. R. (1992). The risk construct. In J. F. Yates (Ed.), *Risk-taking behavior* (pp. 1–25). Wiley.
Zsidisin, G. A., & Wagner, S. M. (2010). Do perceptions become reality? the moderating role of supply chain resiliency on disruption occurrence. *Journal of Business Logistics, 31*(2), 1–20.
Zsidisin GA, Panelli A, Upton R. (2000). Purchasing organization involvement in risk assessments, contingency plans, and risk management: An exploratory study. *Supply Chain Management: An International Journal, 5*(4), 187–198.
Zsidisin, G. A., Petkova, B. N., & Dam, L. (2016). Examining the influence of supply chain glitches on shareholder wealth: Does the reason matter? *International Journal of Production Research, 54*(1), 69–82.

CHAPTER 2

Hurricane Impacts on Supply Chains

Abstract This chapter explores the impact of hurricanes on supply chains and their resulting effects on stock prices. Leveraging event studies and regression analysis, it demonstrates how hurricane-induced disruptions lead to both immediate and long-term financial consequences, often triggering significant market reactions. The analysis highlights the importance of effective Supply Chain Risk Management (SCRM) and the critical role of transparent communication in mitigating these effects. The chapter reveals that detailed damage disclosures can reduce investor uncertainty, leading to more measured stock price responses. This insight underscores the necessity for businesses to prepare and respond strategically to natural disasters.

Keywords Hurricane Impact · Supply Chain Disruption · Stock Price · Financial Impact · Event Study · Supply Chain Risk Management · Investor Reaction · Market Response · Risk Communication · Disaster Management

While the likelihood of a supply chain disruption stemming from a disaster is rare, the repercussions can be substantial when they do occur (Horwich,

P. Schelp et al., *Supply Chain Disruptions and Stock Prices*, Palgrave Studies in Logistics and Supply Chain Management,
https://doi.org/10.1007/978-3-031-68885-0_2

2000). Empirical studies consistently indicate a notable downturn in stock prices following catastrophic events and supply chain disruptions instigated by such events (Brooks et al., 2003; Donadelli & Lucchetta, 2013; Hendricks & Singhal, 2003; Worthington & Valadkhani, 2005; Zsidisin et al., 2016). Utilising regression models like event studies rooted in the efficient market hypothesis, analysts determine the influence of disclosures related to supply chain disruptions on stock returns (Hendricks & Singhal, 2003). These investigations mainly draw quantitative inferences on how supply chain disruptions and stock returns correlate (Hendricks & Singhal, 2003, 2005b; Papadakis, 2006; Zsidisin et al., 2016). Research has also gauged the immediate and long-term effects of these disruptions on stock returns (Caporale & Makarenko, 2019; Hendricks & Singhal, 2005b). A notable 10% reduction in stock prices was observed post the revelation of a supply chain disruption (Hendricks & Singhal, 2003). However, subsequent studies reveal a consistent decline in returns, albeit at reduced magnitudes (Zsidisin et al., 2016).

2.1 Impact of Hurricane-Induced Disruptions on Financial Measures

Natural calamities, especially hurricanes, have an immediate and pronounced influence on corporate stock returns (Brooks et al., 2003; Donadelli & Lucchetta, 2013; Worthington & Valadkhani, 2005). Financial economics delves into the swift aftermaths of these natural tragedies, typically spanning a few trading days (Caporale & Makarenko, 2019; Hendricks & Singhal, 2005b). Instances of extraordinary disturbances, like natural catastrophes, usher in a marked decline in stock returns on the very next trading day (Caporale & Makarenko, 2019). Yet, such studies are diverse, encompassing various disaster types, with hurricanes being just one subset (Brooks et al., 2003; Donadelli & Lucchetta, 2013; Worthington & Valadkhani, 2005).

Research on hurricanes tends to diversify in its scope. Some focus on fiscal aspects like state budgets, revenue streams, and debt (Miao et al., 2018). Others design metrics to approximate financial losses from property damages caused by typhoons (Kim et al., 2019). The ripple effects of hurricanes, exemplified by the 2005 Katrina and Rita, are discerned by studying the stock trajectory of insurance entities (Gangopadhyay et al., 2010).

Supply chain disruptions stemming from unpredictable events, for instance, earthquakes, are associated with notable cumulative abnormal returns (CARs). For example, post the Taiwan earthquake, tech firms witnessed a surge in component costs, which adversely affected their stock prices (Papadakis, 2003, 2006). A nuanced exploration of the literature reveals the varied impact of different natural calamities on firms' financial health across industries. The extent of the fallout is contingent upon the disaster type, but companies across sectors feel the repercussions (Altay & Ramirez, 2010; Corey & Deitch, 2011; Tan & Enderwick, 2006; Worthington & Valadkhani, 2005).

Interestingly, a company does not need to be directly impacted to experience a slump in its stock value. Mere proximity or perceived risk can lead to what's termed as a "contagion effect" (Corey & Deitch, 2011; Filbeck et al., 2016; Kaplanski & Levy, 2010). A similar sentiment is echoed in SCD-related studies where companies merely associated with an impacted entity, either by industry or geography, witness stock volatility (Hobbs et al., 2016; Kaplanski & Levy, 2010).

The magnitude of a disaster does not always align with shareholder reactions. Cases in point include the reactions post the 9/11 attacks, suggesting potential overreactions by the market (Brooks et al., 2003; Donadelli & Lucchetta, 2013; Worthington & Valadkhani, 2005). Overall, the existing literature signifies that supply chain disruptions weigh down stock returns, albeit with differing intensities and duration.

2.1.1 Analysis of Population Data

We study the hurricane impacts on supply chains by scoping the company population based on the country, company's legal form, company's physical supply chain, and time frame. The criteria for selecting observations from the population for this research are detailed as follows:

- **Country:** The research focuses on the United States due to its prominence in industrial production, the plethora of relevant companies, and the strict financial reporting regulations of the US Securities and Exchange Commission (SEC). This ensures an ample amount of public data.
- **Company's Legal Form:** The emphasis is on listed companies as they meet the highest regulatory requirements. This includes regularly updated stock prices, periodic financial reports, and

press releases. Such companies are mandated to disclose significant changes, including unforeseen events or any shifts from their projected strategic objectives, typically along with their reasons.
- **Company's Physical Supply Chain:** As the research pertains to the supply chain domain, the target companies are those listed on the NYSE that rely on a physical supply chain to fulfil their strategic goals. Each company's operations are analysed and the findings are documented.
- **Time frame:** Data from companies listed between 2014 and 2018 is gathered to maintain current relevance and ensure a comprehensive dataset.

2.1.2 Analysis of Hurricane Occurrence

Out of the 2,687 companies listed on NYSE, 625 (or 23%) fit the criteria outlined above, the subsequent section presents a detailed analysis of natural disasters, with a focus on hurricanes, that impacted the selected companies from 2014 to 2018. This analysis was conducted using the R programming language. From the narrowed list of 625 companies, 235 experienced 409 natural disaster events over the five-year period. A significant 38% of these companies encountered at least one such incident, with half of this subset facing multiple disasters. In total, the research encompassed over one million data points.

Figure 2.1 provides a breakdown of the reported natural disaster incidents by category for the years 2014–2018.

The vertical axis in Fig. 2.1 lists the various disaster types in alphabetical order. Each bar graphically represents the total number of occurrences for a specific disaster, with an adjacent percentage indicating its relative frequency among all disaster types. Among the array of natural disasters, hurricanes were predominant, accounting for a substantial 336 incidents or 82% of the total. Other notable disaster types included earthquakes at 7% (or 27 incidents) and droughts at 4% (amounting to 17 incidents).

Figure 2.2 illustrates the frequency of reported hurricane incidents for each company. The y-axis depicts the number of announced hurricane incidents for every firm. Each bar represents the count of companies that reported a specific number of hurricane incidents, and a corresponding percentage beside the bar conveys the fraction of the total companies in

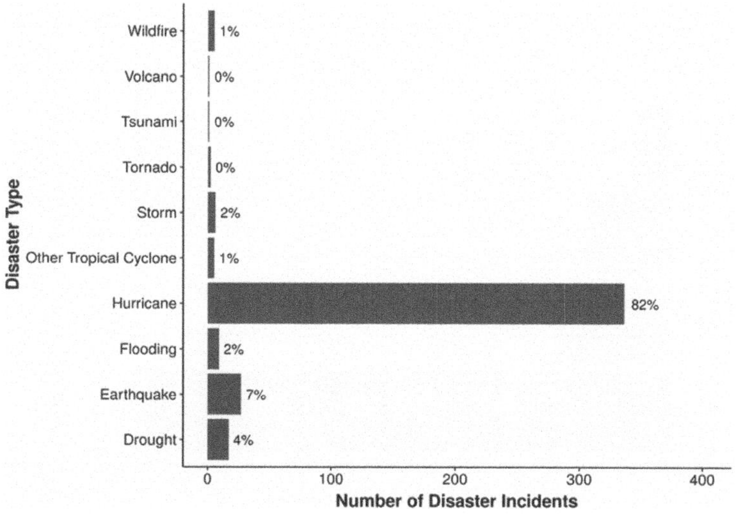

Fig. 2.1 Number of announced natural disaster incidents per disaster type in 2014–2018

that category. Roughly 30% of the target companies experienced hurricane incidents. Among these, half faced a single hurricane, while the remainder endured two, three, or even four hurricanes.

2018 was the second-worst year with around 70 incidents. 2017 (271 hurricane incidents) and 2018 (55 hurricane incidents) were years with massive hurricane damage. In total, more than 350 incidents of natural disaster exposure were recorded for North America which is nearly 90% of all incidents.

Dominance of Hurricanes in Natural Disaster Reports
Of all the companies surveyed, 38% reported experiencing natural disaster episodes between 2014 and 2018. A vast majority, 82%, of these episodes were hurricane-related (please refer to Fig. 2.1). This equates to 30% of the companies having faced the wrath of hurricanes. A closer look reveals that while half of these companies grappled with a single hurricane, the other half braced against recurring events, ranging from two to four encounters. Given that hurricanes, a variant of tropical cyclones, predominantly occur in Latin and North America within specified seasons,

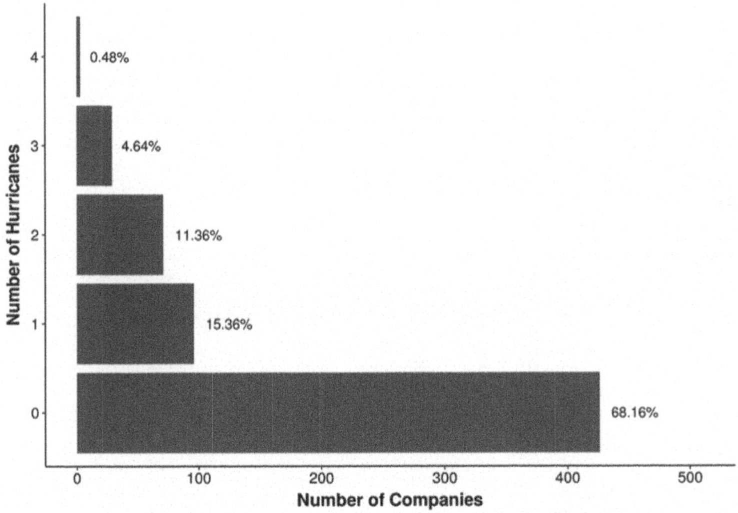

Fig. 2.2 Number of announced hurricane incidents per company

it is coherent that 90% of hurricane events were located in North America. The United States bore the brunt with over 80% of these occurrences.

The years 2017 and 2018 stood out with a surge in hurricane announcements; with 2017 being one of the most economically devastating for the United States due to three significant hurricanes, followed by two major ones in 2018. Therefore, for companies trading on the NYSE, hurricanes can't be dismissed as rare or unpredictable occurrences. Instead, their repeated nature underscores the imperative of strategic planning and adept management responses.

From the overall descriptive analysis, hurricanes have emerged as the most prevalent natural disaster in recent years. The subsequent analysis thus primarily focuses on understanding the implications of hurricane impacts on stock prices.

Influencing Factors

Three main categories of factors may influence a company following a natural disaster: Impact, Actual Damage, and Preventive Measures. The data shows different extents to which companies take preventive closures, either self-imposed or government-mandated.

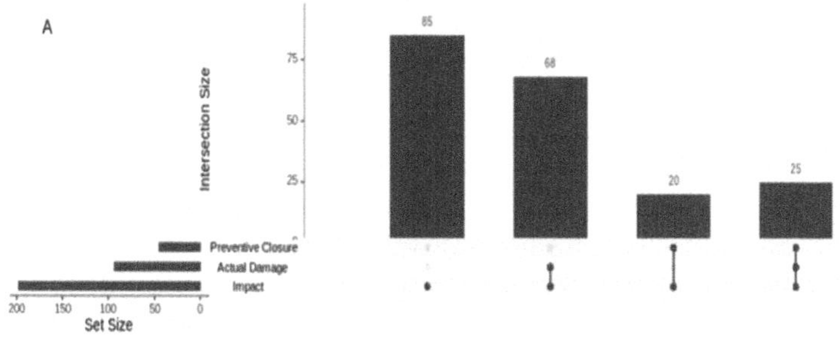

Fig. 2.3 Number of announced hurricane incidents per company

During the process of gathering data, it became evident that the reported influential factors often coexisted, meaning elements like major and minor damages frequently appeared together. Figure 2.3 gives a snapshot of these intertwined events within the potentially influential factors tied to hurricane incidents with three primary categories of influential factors: preventive shutdowns (covering both company facilities and infrastructure), tangible damages, and overall impact, as well as their respective frequency.

A majority of incident reports (85) highlight the impact without delving into details concerning preventive shutdowns or any tangible damages associated with their supply chain. Meanwhile, 86 incidents discuss the impact and detail the damages related to the supply chain. 20 incidents highlight the impact but abstain from providing data on tangible supply chain-related damages, though they do mention preventive closures. On the other hand, 25 companies detail their experience of an impact, revealing both preventive shutdowns and supply chain-related damages.

Every section is divided into two parts: the left side showcases a horizontal bar indicating the total count of reports featuring the subcategories of influential factors. In contrast, the right side enumerates the distinct subcategory reports alongside the intertwined occurrences.

2.1.3 Analysis of Hurricane Impact

Impact categorises the effects of supply chain disruptions, distinguishing between minor and major impacts. Significant impacts are reported in financial statements. Impact is categorised into: (1) Positive demand effect, (2) minor/major supply chain disruption, (3) minor/major other damage.

Figure 2.4 presents a comprehensive overview of the announced factor, "impact". The left section delves into hurricane incidents, whereas the right section addresses other natural disaster events. The y-axis classifies the influencing factors. Each bar chart illustrates instances where the factor was reported (depicted in yellow) against times it wasn't mentioned (shown in grey). The accompanying percentage by each bar signifies the ratio of firms that reported the factor, with the x-axis showing the absolute numbers. Each panel's percentages cumulatively total to 100%.

As highlighted in Fig. 2.4 hurricanes account for 11.1% of incidents causing damage not directly linked to supply chain disruptions, with a significant 77% of these damages being categorised as major. Hurricanes are responsible for 8.4% of all incidents that disrupt the supply chain, with a substantial 57% of these resulting in severe supply chain disruptions.

Figure 2.5 offers a comprehensive breakdown of various impact combinations. Each section is bifurcated into two parts: the left displays a horizontal bar chart that captures the aggregate number of reports featuring the subcategories of influential factors. Concurrently, the right section enumerates both the distinct reports of subcategories and the reports where multiple categories coincide.

The most commonly reported impact in Fig. 2.5, in isolation from other damages, is major non-supply chain-related damages, accounting

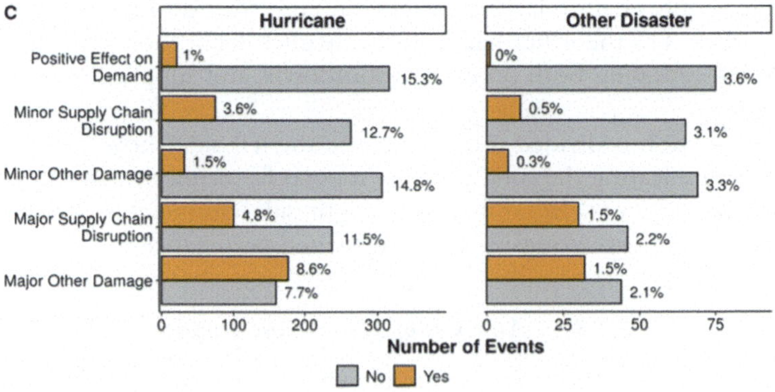

Fig. 2.4 Analysis of announced potentially influencing factor impact

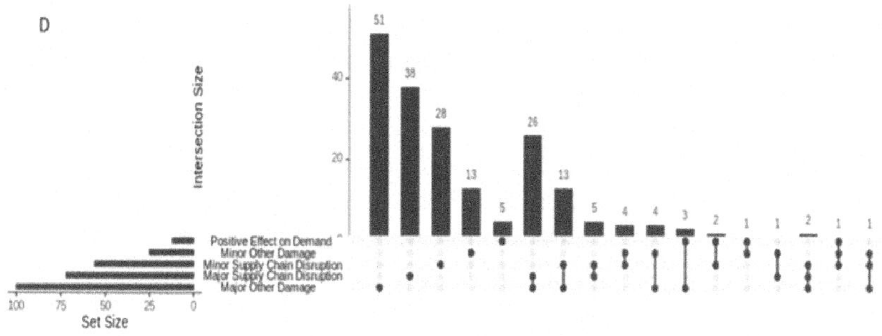

Fig. 2.5 Analysis overlaps of potentially influencing factors within "impact"

for 51%. Examples of this category include damages to structures or a reduction in demand. Following this, the next significant category is major supply chain disruptions, represented in 38 incident reports. When more details are available, these disruptions typically stem from damages to the company's own production facilities. The third most prominent category comprises minor supply chain disruptions (28 incident reports), while the fourth largest (26 incident reports) encompasses companies that reported both major supply chain disruptions and other significant damages.

Evaluating the Impact of Supply Chain Disruptions
Evaluating the impact of supply chain disruptions is not straightforward. The impact of hurricane incident announcement was grouped into two classes: Supply chain disruptions and other damage. Supply chain disruptions were reported for 8% of all announcements. However, it is possible that the category "other damage" contains supply chain damage that was not declared as such. Furthermore, supply chain damage is difficult to demarcate from other damage, in terms of what is still supply chain disruption and what is other damage, e.g., damage to construction facilities.

Other damages are the most reported impact type, with 10%, and comprise a variety of negative effects. One example is the damage to buildings that are not important for the company's actual operations, such as administrative buildings, minor damage to various buildings that do not affect the operations, and rising insurance premiums for buildings. A second example is a decrease in demand for certain goods, which is likely as money will flow into relief operations and reconstruction. In summary, these non-supply chain-related damages can add up, quickly endangering individual financial forecasting.

Grave Consequences of Hurricane Impacts
Hurricane-related repercussions tend to be of a grave nature, with 57% of them leading to Significant Corporate Disruptions and another 59% resulting in various forms of significant damage. This underscores the profound effects hurricanes have on businesses. Not only are most damages attributed to hurricanes, but these damages are also frequently characterised as severe. The consistent reports of considerable other damages and pronounced significant corporate disruptions are anticipated since regulatory stipulations necessitate companies to disclose such critical impacts. When a company reports substantial supply chain disruption or extensive other damages, the implications are often so dire that noting additional minor damages becomes inconsequential.

2.1.4 Analysis of Hurricane Damage

Hurricanes, in particular, pose substantial risks to supply chains, especially in regions prone to tropical storms. The impact of hurricanes on supply chains can be profound, leading to disruptions in transportation, production, and distribution. Key factors contributing to supply chain vulnerabilities during hurricanes include:

- **Transportation Disruptions:** Hurricanes can damage transportation infrastructure, including roads, ports, and airports, making it challenging to move goods within and between regions.
- **Production Halts:** Manufacturing facilities in hurricane-prone areas may be forced to halt operations to ensure employee safety and protect assets from damage.
- **Supplier and Customer Disruptions:** Suppliers and customers within the hurricane-affected area may face their own challenges, leading to delays and interruptions in the supply chain.
- **Inventory Shortages:** Supply chain partners may experience inventory shortages due to transportation disruptions, production halts, or increased demand for disaster-related goods.

- **Communication Breakdowns:** Hurricanes can disrupt communication systems, making it difficult for supply chain partners to coordinate and respond effectively.

Given the potential for substantial supply chain disruptions, businesses must proactively manage the risks associated with hurricanes and other natural disasters. This includes developing contingency plans, diversifying supplier sources, and investing in technology and infrastructure that enhances supply chain resilience (Blackhurst et al., 2005; Sheffi & Rice Jr., 2005; Tang, 2006).

Actual damage includes direct harm to facilities or infrastructure, affecting production and operations. Hurricanes lead to storm and flood damage that can impact companies' supply chain-related infrastructure, causing potential reductions in production or complete shutdowns of facilities. Some damages, like those in agriculture, can cause supply chain disruptions in specific sectors, such as the food industry.

In this research actual damage was categorised into (1) disruptions at suppliers, (2) harm to own sites, (3) damage to infrastructure, and (4) agricultural damage. Figure 2.6 provides a detailed breakdown of the announced factor "actual damage".

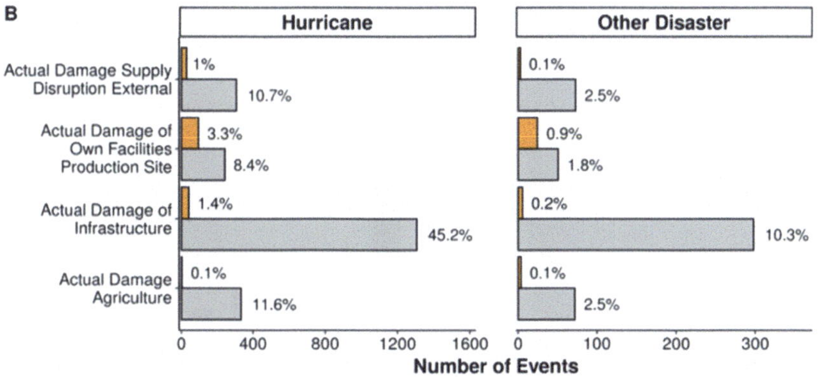

Fig. 2.6 Descriptive analysis of announced potentially influencing factor vs actual damage

The left side of Fig. 2.6 presents data on hurricane incidents, while the right side addresses other natural disaster occurrences. The influencing factors are presented as "Hurricane" and "Other Disaster". The bar charts display the number of incidents where the factor was reported (shown in yellow) and instances where the factor was not mentioned (in grey). The percentage alongside each bar indicates the proportion of firms announcing the factor, with the x-axis detailing the absolute values. The combined percentages in each panel total 100%.

Regarding hurricane-related damages, the most common are as follows: Damage to a company's production facilities accounting for 4.2% of all natural disaster incidents. Infrastructure damage contributing to over 1.6% of all incidents. External supply chain disruptions from upstream suppliers making up 1.1% of the incidents.

Figure 2.7 illustrates that the most commonly reported incident is exclusive damage to a company's own production facilities, with 53 such instances. The left section features a horizontal bar summarising the aggregate of reports within the influencing factor subcategories. The right segment details the individual subcategory reports and also highlights where these reports have overlapped.

Frequently, reports combine damages to both the company's facilities and the broader infrastructure. In Fig. 2.7, a subset of nine incidents focusing on external supply chain disruptions does not detail any direct damages. Meanwhile, eight incidents specify only infrastructure damage,

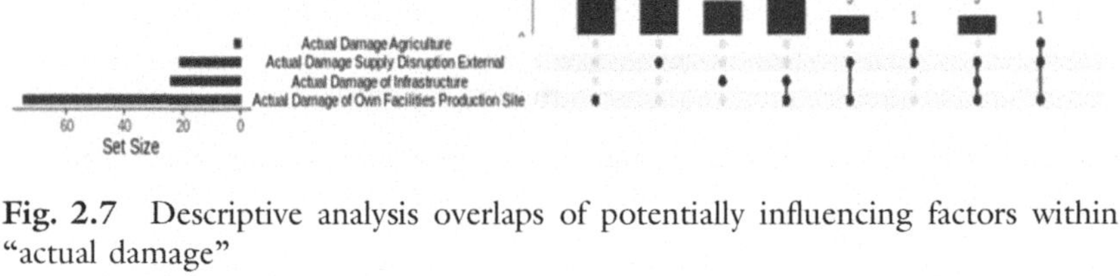

Fig. 2.7 Descriptive analysis overlaps of potentially influencing factors within "actual damage"

such as to ports, airports, and electricity, without mentioning any direct harm to the company's assets.

Geographic Closeness to Hurricanes Influences Damage Outcomes
Often, damages impacted both company facilities and infrastructure, reflecting the regional force of hurricanes. Strategic Supply Chain Risk Management can mitigate these effects, like planning alternative transport routes. Some reported infrastructure damages without significant supply chain disruptions possibly due to effective supply chain risk management strategies. While some firms were not in the hurricane's immediate vicinity, their suppliers were. Proactive supply chain risk management, like diversifying supplier locations, could prevent such disruptions.

Aggregated and Delayed Reporting of Hurricane Damage
Most firms announced hurricane damage on the last day of the hurricane or later. This is not surprising as companies need time to assess the exact damage. Often firms reported on hurricane incidents in their next quarterly or annual report.

A substantial ratio of 53% of the announcements report damage from two or more hurricanes. Hurricanes follow a seasonal pattern and occur in close temporal proximity or even overlap. Companies might report the damage of hurricanes in an aggregated way in their financial reports as the damage per hurricane is not very severe, but the accumulated damage is. Reporting of incidents on the same date implies a shared anchor, resulting in higher uncertainty, because the damage allocation per hurricane on stock price can be more challenging.

2.2 Stock Price Prediction Model

This research assesses how stock prices, tracked over a period, are impacted by hurricane announcements using an interrupted time series analysis (ITSA) method (Lagarde, 2012). The approach involves two main phases as shown in Fig. 2.8:

Phase 1: Estimation of ARIMA model parameters (Box & Tiao, 1975).
Phase 2: ITSA which identifies when these hurricane interruptions occur.

The ARIMA model, known for its prowess in financial forecasting and various other domains like tourism, was selected to represent stock prices using a 12-month prelude to hurricane announcements (Ariyo et al., 2014; Cho, 2001; Hyndman & Athanasopoulos, 2018). It accounts for stock price patterns such as trends, seasonality, and autocorrelations.

The ITSA method delves into how hurricane announcements disrupt stock prices, pinpointing the exact moments, termed "anchors" in this study, and assessing their implications (Helfenstein, 1991).

The choice of the ARIMA-intervention model owes to its robustness, evidenced in cases like the post-2008 downturn in China's manufacturing (Chung et al., 2009). Combining ARIMA's predictive capabilities with ITSA's flexibility allows for a comprehensive examination of both transient and enduring effects of interruptions, making its application to natural disaster-induced stock price disruptions particularly innovative (Beard et al., 2019).

The probability of a disaster-originated supply chain disruption is low; however, if it occurs it may be very costly (Horwich, 2000). The efficient market hypothesis assumes that in an efficient market new information such as the announcement of a supply chain disruption will be immediately reflected in the share price (Fama et al., 1969; Hendricks & Singhal, 2003). Past study results confirm the theory: a 10% decrease in stock price of listed companies was identified after the announcement of a supply chain disruption (Hendricks & Singhal, 2003, 2008). More

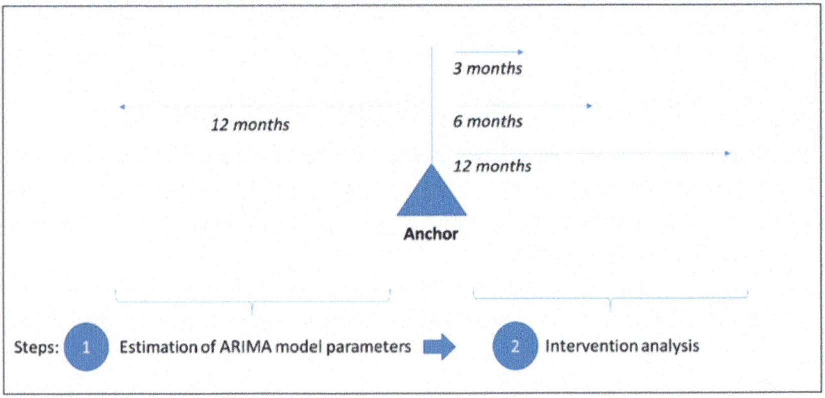

Fig. 2.8 Time series analysis: steps of model creation and fitting

recent studies confirmed a significant drop in stock price returns, but with smaller impacts (Zsidisin et al., 2016). Supply chain disruptions caused by natural uncertainty and natural disasters such as an earthquake were linked to significant CARs (Papadakis, 2006).

The impact on firms by force majeure events, specifically natural disasters, was found to be mirrored by an immediate, significant negative effect on stock price returns for the first trading day (Caporale & Makarenko, 2019). On this basis Hypothesis 1 is deduced.

H1: *Hurricane announcements influence stock prices.*

Not just firm announcements but also the general hurricane announcement is tested to be able to compare investors' reactions to risk (a hurricane incident announcement) with the reaction to an uncertainty (e.g., hurricane landfall). This is supported by the contagion theory, which describes the spreading of market reaction to companies of the same industry or at the same location as reflected by their stock price value, even though they are not affected by the event themselves (Filbeck et al., 2016). As risk researchers in decision theory and finance argue that risk is not just the downside, but also the upside possibility (Arrow, 1970; Kahneman & Tversky, 1979; Rao & Goldsby, 2009; Wagner & Bode, 2008). In past studies some firms had positive effects, e.g., due to increased demand. Therefore, in the hypothesis the word "effect" is used, which includes upside and downside risk.

Anchors: In this context, an anchor represents the point of interruption. Two main anchors are tested:

Anchor A: The Reveal of Firm-specific Information

Anchor A represents the time when information about a hurricane incident related to a specific firm becomes public. If this date isn't a trading day, the next trading day is taken (López-de Lacalle, 2016).

Anchor B: Hurricane Announcement

Anchor B includes announcements that are related to a certain hurricane but that are not linked to a firm. We explain this anchor in detail later.

Outcome Variable: The variable in focus, Y_{it}, signifies the stock price for approximately 625 companies over time. Data for this is sourced from NYSE using Yahoo Finance's API, with emphasis on the closing value each trading day. The analysis is centred around the date of the hurricane announcement, spanning one year before and after it. Companies with insufficient data are excluded from the study.

In summary, hurricane announcements influence stock prices. These announcements could have three types of effects:

- **Pulse effect:** Announcements may lead to a short-lived impact on stock prices.
- **Step effect:** Announcements may result in a lasting impact on stock prices.
- **Transitory effect:** Announcements may create a brief change in stock prices.

These three effects are shown in Fig. 2.9.

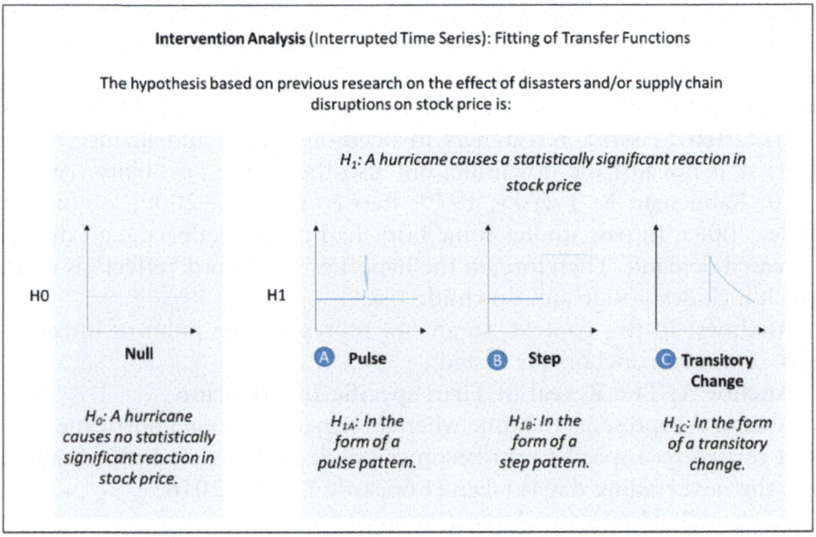

Fig. 2.9 Transfer functions capturing the effects of announcements

2.2.1 *The Effect of Incident Announcement on Stock Price*

Stock price allows measurement of the subjective risk perceived by the shareholders and thereby allows measurement of the risk, and translates it into an objective risk view (Khan & Burnes, 2007; Zsidisin & Wagner, 2010). The perception of investors, which is subjective, is reflected by the objective measurement of stock price in a specific pattern. Thereby the identification of different patterns is important to reverse engineer the perceived subjective risk origin. One study found, for example, that investors react differently to disasters depending on whether they were anticipated or unanticipated (Brooks et al., 2003). Apparently, investors react more slowly to unanticipated events than to scheduled events, probably because they need time to form an opinion on the subjective risks.

Hurricanes can be seen as somewhat scheduled; however, they can change their path and their impact can be difficult to determine. It would be interesting to see how quickly investors react to different hurricane information or impact statements. Reactions of stock prices after an interruption such as a hurricane can be measured by transfer functions in the form of a pulse, a step, or a transitory change function of the time series (Box & Tiao, 1975).

Certain stock price patterns can also be an indicator of psychological phenomena: a pulse pattern supports the overreaction hypothesis which suggests that investors and security analysts tend to overreact to good and bad news mirrored by the estimation of earnings, resulting in an unjustifiable stock price reaction (De Bondt, 1993; De Bondt & Thaler, 1990; Filbeck et al., 2016). Study results support overreactions: a significant negative reaction occurs on the day of and the day after an announcement of a supply chain disruption (Filbeck et al., 2016; Hendricks & Singhal, 2003). Similarly, negative returns after force majeure events are in most cases observed on the day of the event (Caporale & Makarenko, 2019). A 10% decrease in the stock price of listed companies is found after the announcement of a supply chain disruption (Hendricks & Singhal, 2003, 2008); however, more recent studies show smaller impacts such as 1.94% (Zsidisin et al., 2016). A significant long-term reaction was found: a decrease in stock price returns is found in the year after a supply chain disruption (Hendricks & Singhal, 2005a). Although a significant negative relationship between supply chain disruptions and stock price returns has been established, the magnitude and duration of the observed effects differ (Hendricks & Singhal, 2003; Zsidisin et al., 2016); therefore, Hypothesis 1 is split into three sub-hypotheses to test the nature of the stock price reaction. Figure 2.9 shows the null hypothesis and the main hypothesis and its sub-hypotheses together with the transfer functions representing these. Pulse function (A) lasts one day; step function (B) and transitory change function (C) last longer than one trading day.

The sub-hypotheses of H1 are as follows:

H1a: *A hurricane incident announcement/hurricane announcement has a short-term effect on stock price defined as a pulse function.*

H1b: *A hurricane incident announcement/hurricane announcement has a persisting effect on stock price defined as a step function.*

H1c: *A hurricane incident announcement/hurricane announcement has a transient effect on stock price defined as a transitory change function.*

2.2.2 *Intervention Analysis*

Figure 2.10 reveals that 25–31% of the firms studied experienced significant stock price changes due to hurricane disruptions. However, 69–75% of the firms did not show a noticeable reaction. This response remains consistent across various time frames (3, 6, and 12 months), indicating that disruptions persist over time.

Figure 2.11 breaks down the type of stock price reaction. Around 70% of the significant stock price disruptions are best characterised as transitory changes.

In Fig. 2.11, both step and pulse effects account for about 15% each. The direction of the stock price reactions (whether they increase or decrease) is colour-coded, with red indicating a negative reaction and green indicating a positive reaction.

Figure 2.12 presents the intensity and direction of stock price changes due to hurricane announcements. Both positive and negative changes were observed, with persistent changes (step function) exhibiting the

Fig. 2.10 Results of the ARIMA-intervention model for Anchor A

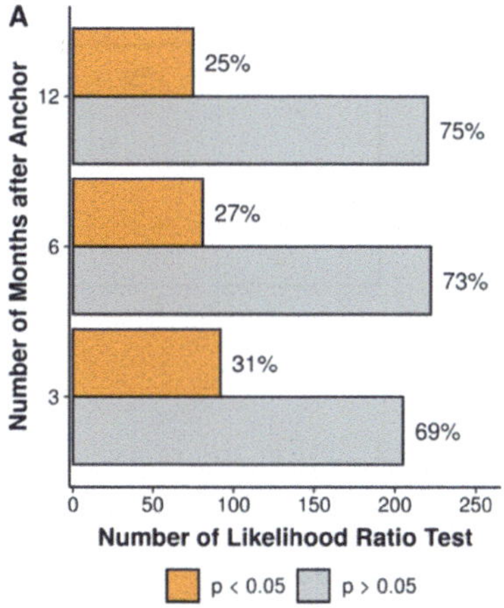

Fig. 2.11 Distribution of observations to transfer functions

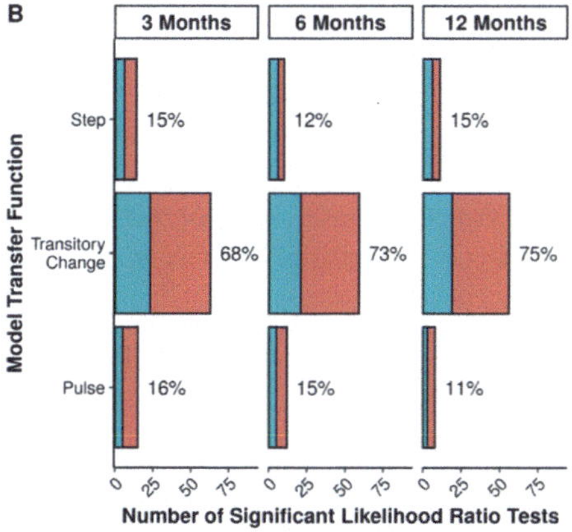

most pronounced shifts. Reactions described as transitory changes display the most intense positive and negative effects across all time frames.

Figure 2.13 visually demonstrates that both positive and negative stock price effects diminish over time. While the decay is still ongoing when the 3-month window after the hurricane announcement is analysed, it is almost complete when a 12-month window is considered. The left panel in Fig. 2.13 shows that the decay has not yet reached zero for several

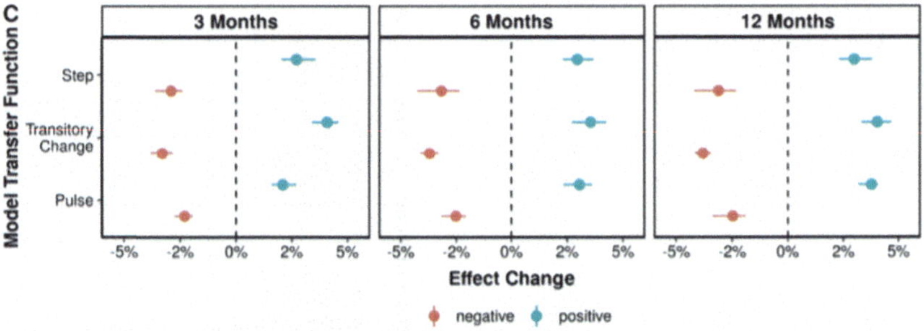

Fig. 2.12 Effect size of each transfer function

observations within the 3-month window after the anchor, while in the right panel all decays reach near zero.

In Fig. 2.14, an omega value closer to 1 indicates a faster decay, while a value closer to 0.5 suggests a more persistent effect. The results indicate that stock price reactions to hurricanes, whether positive or negative, fade relatively quickly with omega values around 0.8 and 0.9.

In summary, while hurricane announcements have a noticeable effect on some firms' stock prices, the majority do not exhibit a significant reaction. Among those that do, most reactions are transient, with stock prices eventually returning to their original levels.

Fig. 2.13 Effect decay over time

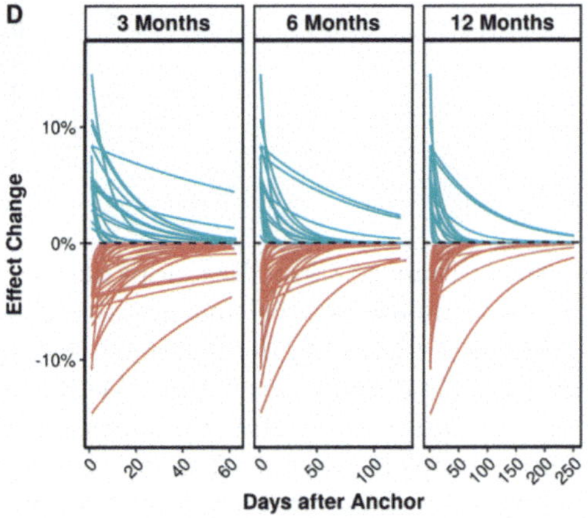

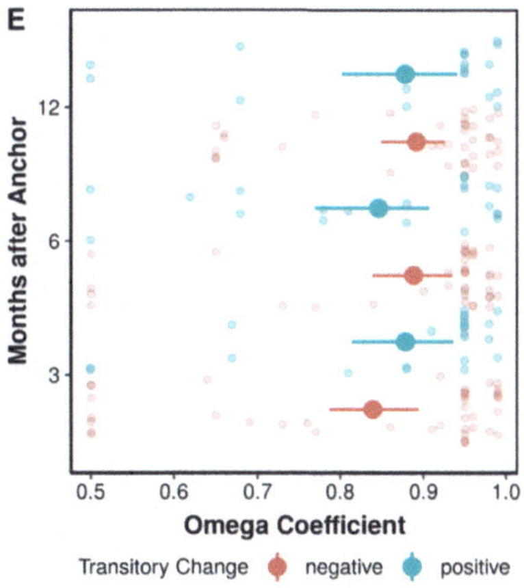

Fig. 2.14 Decay speed

Stock Price Reacts to Hurricane Announcements (H1). About 25–31% of the time, hurricane-related announcements significantly impact firm stock prices, predominantly negative.

Stock Price Changes Over Time (H1a, b, c). In approximately 70% of instances, stock price effects are transitory, with both positive and negative shifts diminishing over time, suggesting a combination of initial overreaction and sustained response.

2.2.3 Stock Price Reaction to Hurricane Announcements

Hypothesis 1 posits that hurricane-related announcements significantly affect stock prices, echoing the efficient market hypothesis (Kahneman & Tversky, 1973). Stock prices reflect the shareholders' perceived risk, translating subjective assessments into objective views (Khan & Burnes, 2007; Zsidisin & Wagner, 2010).

For hurricane incident announcements, around 30% of firms' announcements led to noticeable stock price disruptions on the announcement day, consistent with the efficient market hypothesis and supported by previous studies (Caporale & Makarenko, 2019; Hendricks & Singhal, 2008; Zsidisin et al., 2016). These disruptions remain stable over extended periods, from three to twelve months. More negative extremes in stock price reactions were observed, especially when companies reported damage from back-to-back hurricanes, mainly Harvey and Irma. Notably, firms experienced these extreme reactions due to aggregated hurricane reports. Most cases (over 60%) align with a transitory change function, with negative stock price effects dissipating more quickly than positive ones. This fade may arise from repair works post-hurricane damage and investors' fading memory of the incident. In essence, hurricane incidents typically lead to a sharp negative stock price response that diminishes over time, corroborating prior research findings.

Hurricane incident announcements tend to lead to predominantly negative stock price reactions. This is in line with earlier studies that identified adverse impacts of disasters or supply chain disruptions on stock prices (Caporale & Makarenko, 2019; Hendricks & Singhal, 2003, 2008; Papadakis, 2006; Zsidisin et al., 2016). These findings align with the efficient market hypothesis, which posits that markets swiftly adjust to new information (Fama et al., 1969). The study introduced transfer functions to profile stock price reaction patterns. The most recurrent pattern was the transitory change function, indicating a temporary yet sharp reaction, supporting the overreaction hypothesis.

As a methodological advancement, three different time spans (3, 6, and 12 months) were tested, and the results were consistently robust across these periods.

In conclusion, hurricanes are not black swan events but frequently occurring phenomena that cause harm to businesses in several forms and tend to lead to a negative reaction of stock price in the case of listed firms.

Hurricane risk has to be actively managed by firms. Disasters cannot be avoided; therefore, firms have to be prepared. Supply chain disruptions can have a significant impact on firm performance; this is especially the case when the disruptions are disaster-induced. Stock price—one measure of firm performance—is likely to be affected after the announcement of a hurricane incident. But a company does not even need to suffer damage or publish damage to have its stock price affected, due to contagion effects.

A firm's stock price may be affected if a hurricane or hurricane landfall is predicted or announced. Just the information on a hurricane and the uncertainty regarding potential future damage can induce a shareholder reaction. Investors fear potential damage, or, when the hurricane already hit, are hesitant to invest in the business further when little or no information is provided about the severity of the hurricane damage. Therefore, companies need to communicate as soon as possible with their shareholders providing details of the damage.

The stock price effect is mostly described by a transitory function indicating an overreaction component followed by a return to normality over time. To prevent or reduce this overreaction, companies that are not affected are advised to publish an announcement to inform their shareholders and stakeholders that the company is not affected, as this will be beneficial to manage the negative reaction of stock prices to hurricane news.

2.3 Impact Type and Effect

The influence of hurricanes or associated supply chain interruptions varies based on the field of study. While SCM studies emphasise the effects of supply chain disruptions, economic research zeroes in on other types of damages. Researchers in financial economics often consider non-supply chain damages, such as a fall in demand, damage to assets, or a rise in insurance costs. They may also analyse the aggregate consequences of a disaster, including damages stemming from supply chain disruptions (Donadelli & Lucchetta, 2013).

2.3.1 Supply Chain Disruption vs Other Types of Impact

Broadly speaking, catastrophes like hurricanes typically result in adverse outcomes (Donadelli & Lucchetta, 2013). Similarly, supply chain disruptions are observed to have a notable negative influence on stock prices. Supply chain studies typically overlook firm announcements that state impacts other than SCDs, especially if an SCD is not the sole damaging factor. Since no single study currently offers a direct comparison, this book ascertains if the stock price response varies based on whether the reported impact is an SCD or another form of damage. This leads to the proposed hypothesis:

H2: *The nature of the impact (whether it's a supply chain disruption or a different kind of damage) shapes the stock price response following an announcement about a hurricane event.*

This hypothesis was evaluated in the context of hurricane incident announcements denoted by Anchor A. Figure 2.15 showcases the findings from the intervention analysis when classifying announcements based on impact types (major SCD, major other damage, minor SCD, and minor other damage).

From the results, each impact type introduces interruptions across all time spans, ranging between 16% and 38%. Both major other damage and major SCDs consistently display interruptions across all periods, with roughly 30% marking the highest frequency of disruption. Interestingly, minor other damages exhibit 34% disruptions over a three-month span, but this decreases to approximately 20% for both six and twelve-month durations. In contrast, minor SCDs and the positive impacts on demand consistently present a 20% interruption across all temporal frames.

In Fig. 2.15, the number of Likelihood Ratio Tests (LRT) for the following categories are depicted: major other damage, major SCD, minor other damage, minor SCD, and positive demand effects. For every unique pairing of company and hurricane incident announcement, the ARIMA-intervention model with the most minimal Akaike Information Criterion (AIC) value is selected. If the p-value of the LRT, which contrasts a baseline model devoid of interventions against one with interventions, falls below the standard 0.05 threshold, the modelled disruption is deemed statistically significant, represented in orange. The percentages depict the fraction of statistically valid LRTs for each bar.

Figure 2.16 depicts the optimal transfer function based on statistically relevant likelihood ratio tests. It visualises the nature and direction of interruptions for different firm types in relation to hurricane incident announcements.

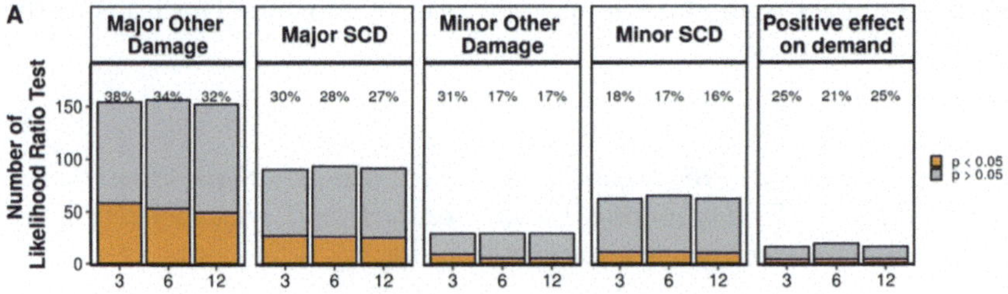

Fig. 2.15 Impact types and their significance for stock price changes

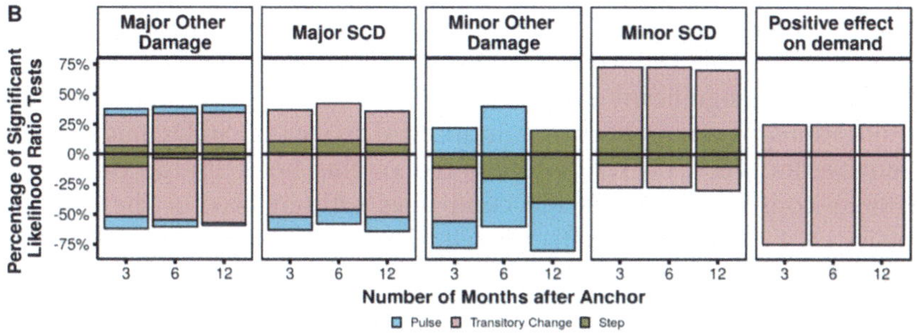

Fig. 2.16 Impact types versus transfer functions

In Fig. 2.16, every time span's data sums up to 100%. For each duration, the graph highlights which of the three primary transfer functions—step (in rose), transitory change (in olive), or pulse (in light blue)—best fits the statistically significant LRT results. The bars represent the most suitable function for the model, gauged by a significant LRT and the lowest AIC, for specific firms and their hurricane events. Negative responses are shown by the bars beneath the 0 line, while positive ones are displayed above it.

2.3.2 Stock Price Response to Magnitude of Impact

As a third hypothesis, the Magnitude of Impact was tested. The goal of SCRM is to mitigate risks, like SCDs (Wieland & Wallenburg, 2012). Studies have determined that companies with a robust SCRM focus are less susceptible and demonstrate superior supply chain outcomes. Both SCM and the resulting performance of the supply chain influence financial results (Wahdan et al., 2017). As a result, one could posit that a minimal SCD impact would correlate with minor shifts in financial performance, manifested as stock price variations. This aligns with the efficient market hypothesis, which proposes that fresh data, such as updates on SCD impacts, will instantly affect stock prices. Thus, stock prices are believed to mirror the present informational landscape available to investors (Fama et al., 1969). Given this, investors might have a more tempered reaction to news of smaller SCDs, viewing them as indicators of effective SCRM (Ellis et al., 2011; Wagner & Neshat, 2012).

Most research on supply chain risks and disruptions revolves around unexpected, significant events that are mandated to be publicly disclosed. The focus on significant events in academic writings suggests that the ramifications of minor hurricane-induced damages or SCDs might have been overlooked. The results presented in this book bridge this oversight by considering events and companies without bias for the scale of impact or if a hurricane's effect is felt. These considerations lead to the subsequent hypothesis:

H3: *The magnitude of the impact (whether minor or significant) shapes the stock price response after a hurricane event announcement.*

Figure 2.17 shows the effect change of step, pulse, and transitory function for the three time horizons per group. The effect changes left of the zero line have negative transfer function coefficients (circle shape) and right of the zero line have positive (triangle shape) ones.

In Fig. 2.17, major damages show more negative effects of a transient nature on the stock price. Interestingly, minor other damages have the largest proportion of persistent large negative effects for the 12-month time horizon (negative step function).

Furthermore, minor supply chain disruptions lead to a higher proportion of positive effects on stock prices with the second largest percentage change in Fig. 2.17, while all positive effects on demand are short-lived.

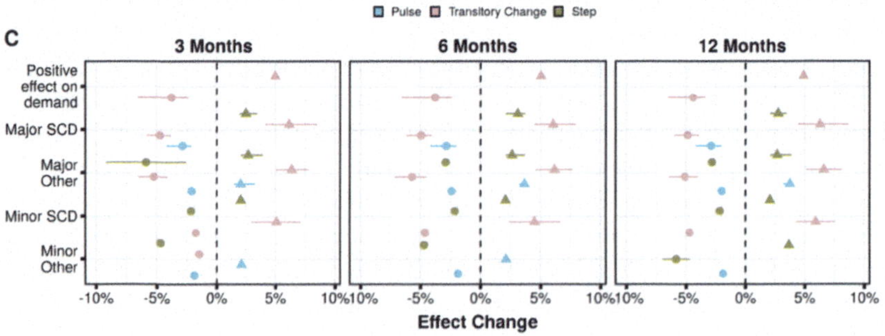

Fig. 2.17 Impact types and effect size for each transfer function

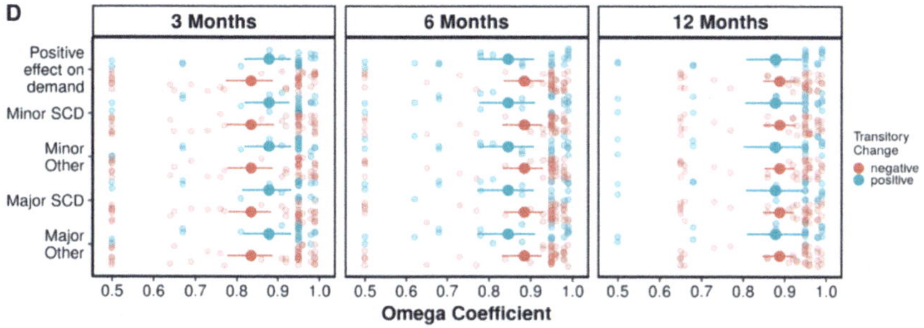

Fig. 2.18 Omega coefficient showing the transitory change

Figure 2.18 presents the omega coefficient for the transitory change transfer functions across the three time frames for each group. An omega coefficient nearing 1.0 indicates a faster diminishing effect, aligning closer to the pulse function. Conversely, an omega coefficient closer to 0.5 leans towards a step function.

To sum up, while negative impacts are more common for major and minor other damages as well as major supply chain disruptions, these effects wane a bit quicker than positive ones, as illustrated in Fig. 2.18.

In terms of the type of impact, we observe that approximately a quarter of incidents result in notable stock price fluctuations due to both supply chain disruptions and other damages. However, other damages appear to prompt a greater percentage of significant reactions compared to supply chain disruptions.

In terms of the magnitude of impact (i.e., major vs minor impact), generally, the information about the impact seems to be the primary driver for a marked stock price change, more so than the details on damage or preventive actions. While the severity of the impact (be it major or minor) dictates the frequency of significant stock price changes, it does not necessarily determine the overall trend, such as whether the reactions are positive or negative.

In H2, we hypothesise that stock price reactions are influenced by the nature of the impact (be it supply chain disruption or other types of damage) due to hurricane incident announcements.

In H3, we hypothesise that the severity of the impact, whether minor or major, shapes the stock price reaction following a hurricane incident announcement.

We examine both these hypotheses concurrently due to their interconnected nature. Hypothesis 2 postulates that the type of impact, whether from supply chain disruptions or other damages, affects stock prices. This investigation aligns with past supply chain management studies that identified stock price variations resulting from supply chain disruptions and, drawing parallels with financial economics research, from broader disasters. Approximately 20–30% of firms included in the analysis showed time series disruptions when faced with these impacts, substantiating H2.

Notably, the results suggested that the specific nature of the impact, such as supply chain disruption or alternate damages, was not as influential on stock prices as the severity of the impact, which was explored in H3. According to H3, the magnitude of the impact determines its influence on stock prices. This aligns with the efficient market hypothesis, which proposes that new, pertinent information, like reports on the effects of supply chain disruptions, would swiftly reflect in stock prices. More pronounced impacts, like significant supply chain disruptions or other major damages, were most likely to interrupt stock prices. This underscores the belief that investors quickly adjust to fresh data and may view minor supply chain disruptions as evidence of effective supply chain risk management.

Both major impact categories manifested similar reactions from investors, emphasising that the prime consideration for investors might not be the nature of the damage but its magnitude. For instance, initial investor reactions to property damage or declining demand might be severe, but this could be transient as they later recognise insurance safeguards and potential demand normalisation post-disaster recovery.

Interestingly, major supply chain disruptions also generated comparable reactions, where about 30% of affected firms experienced stock price disruptions that remained consistent over time. Predominantly negative, these reactions may signify investors penalising perceived inadequacies in supply chain management. Past research confirms this negative bias, though the fleeting nature of these effects varies across studies.

Over time, investors either downplay the incident, become more informed about damage recovery, or see the situation as less perilous. In sum, while negative consequences are dominant for both major and minor damages, they wane more swiftly than their positive counterparts. Typically, the proportion of firms facing interruptions remains consistent, irrespective of the time frame considered. The predominant pattern leans towards a transitory change function, hinting at possible investor overreactions or the incident fading from memory. On the flip side, sustained positive effects could bolster shareholder confidence. In a broader perspective, some firms even derive benefits from hurricane incidents, an aspect often overshadowed in prior research. In essence, the impact's magnitude holds more sway than its type.

Exploring the impact types and their scales, the study both reaffirms previous findings and offers new insights. Announcements of supply chain disruptions and other damages significantly affect stock prices. Major supply chain disruptions tend to depress stock prices, yet minor supply chain disruptions frequently lead to a rise. This novel observation implies that shareholders recognise and value efficient supply chain risk management that can prevent larger issues. Conversely, damages not tied to supply chain disruptions, such as those stemming from natural disasters, predominantly result in negative stock price reactions, consistent with prior research.

From a practical standpoint, companies disclosing hurricane-related events must anticipate stock price reactions. While major supply chain disruptions are generally detrimental to stock prices, minor ones can prove beneficial, underscoring the significance of supply chain risk management. Corporate leadership and boards are thus encouraged to prioritise SCRM strategies, especially given that damages not linked to the supply chain, irrespective of their scale, often lead to stock price downturns. This combined analysis provides both theoretical insights and actionable recommendations for businesses.

2.4 Nature of Damage

Disasters vary in their nature and extent of damage (Dietch & Corey, 2011). When evaluating the effects of hurricanes, academic research delves deeper into the specifics of supply chain disruptions and other associated damages, offering insights that can be quantitatively analysed. Supply chain disruptions may arise from internal operational challenges within a company or be a consequence of supplier failures or transportation issues (Dietch & Corey, 2011). Numerous organisations grapple with significant infrastructure failures, often exacerbated by the unavailability of essential utilities like gas and electricity (Boin & McConnell, 2007). Beyond supply chain disruptions, hurricanes can induce various other damages, such as harm to non-manufacturing structures or the loss of employees and clientele (Dietch & Corey, 2011). Both academic studies in the fields of business and economics and official reports (e.g., regarding Hurricane Harvey from the National Hurricane Center in 2017) shed light on these damages. Yet, the impact of these diverse damage types on stock prices remains unexplored. Historically, data collection in studies typically permitted only binary evaluations, focusing on the presence or absence of damage without differentiation by damage types. Based on these observations, the ensuing hypothesis is proposed:

H4: *The nature and extent of actual damage shape the stock price response following an announcement about a hurricane-related event.*

2.4.1 Preventive Closures and Actual Damage Announcements

Figure 2.19 presents the count of LRTs for impact, actual damage, and preventive closures. For each pairing of a company with a hurricane incident announcement, the ARIMA-intervention model that has the lowest AIC is taken into account. If the LRT's p-value, when comparing a model without any intervention to one with an intervention, falls below the set significance level of 0.05 threshold, then the interruption depicted in the model is deemed statistically significant, marked by an orange colour. The represented percentages on the graph indicate the ratio of these significant LRTs in each bar.

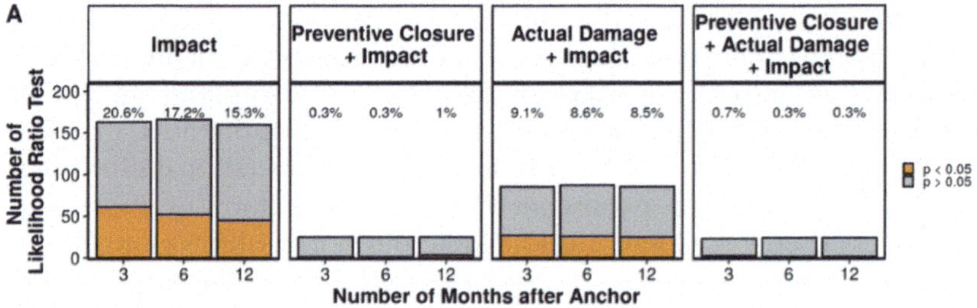

Fig. 2.19 Preventive closures, actual damage, and impact announcements

The LRT counts in Fig. 2.19 are graphically represented for several combinations: impact alone, impact combined with preventive closure, impact combined with actual damage, and a three-way combination of impact, actual damage, and preventive closure. Descriptive analysis suggested that these combinations were the most frequently occurring, hence offering ample data for effective testing.

From Fig. 2.19, it becomes evident that for the group combinations of preventive closure with impact, and preventive closure combined with actual damage and impact, there aren't enough significant LRTs to further delineate positive from negative reactions. Consequently, only the impact and the combined impact with actual damage are detailed in subsequent panels.

In most instances, the transitory change function emerges as the optimal fitting transfer function, as demonstrated in Fig. 2.20. This figure visualises the transfer function and the direction of interruptions based on the company type and specific hurricane incident announcements.

For clarity, each time span represented in Fig. 2.20 sums up to 100%. Within these time frames, the best-fitting proportions of significant LRTs are depicted as comprehensive bars. These bars are segmented into three primary transfer functions: step (depicted in rose), transitory change (in olive), and pulse (in light blue). Each bar is representative of the most suitable transfer function based on the model that has a noteworthy LRT and the lowest AIC, tailored to the specific firm and its corresponding hurricane incidents.

To differentiate, negative reactions are illustrated by bars located below the 0 line, while positive ones are represented above this line.

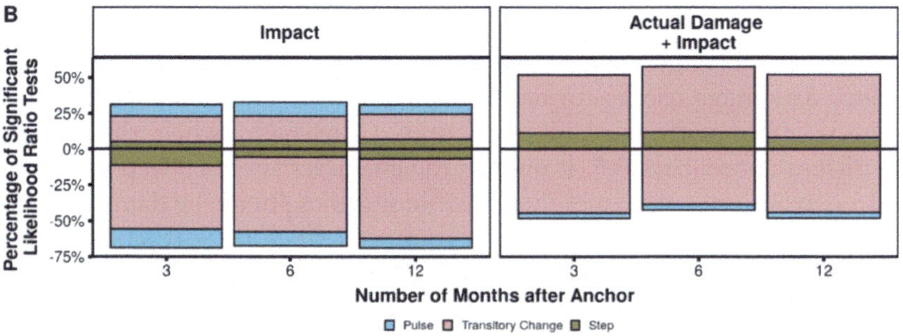

Fig. 2.20 Comparison of impact with impact and actual damage

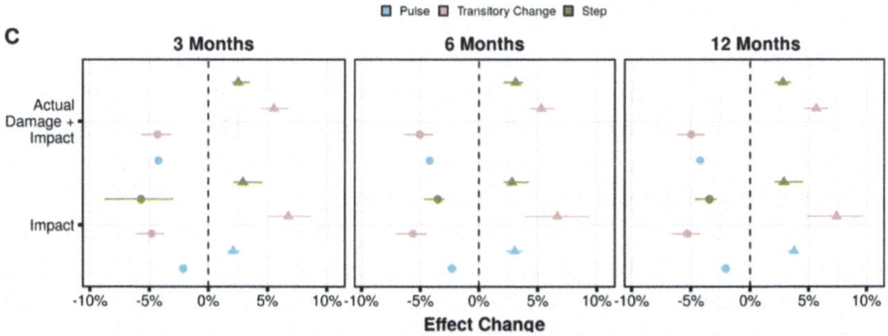

Fig. 2.21 Comparison of impact with impact and actual damage in terms of effect change

Figure 2.21 visualises the alteration in effect for step, pulse, and transitory functions across the three time intervals for each group. Effects to the left of the zero line are marked by negative transfer function coefficients (depicted as circles), while those to the right are characterised by positive coefficients (represented as triangles).

When considered individually, the impact exhibited a greater proportion of negative consequences compared to when paired with actual damage. Yet, the relative alteration in stock price maintained a consistent magnitude regardless of the transfer function, especially when viewed over a 12-month span post-anchor. While the solo impact displayed an increased frequency of negative consequences through a transitory transfer function, as illustrated in Fig. 2.20, these effects dissipated more rapidly than their positive counterparts at the 6 or 12-month marks, as highlighted in Fig. 2.22.

Figure 2.22 displays the omega coefficient values for the transitory change transfer functions across three different time frames for each group. An omega coefficient nearing 1.0 indicates a quicker fading effect, aligning more with the pulse function. Conversely, when the omega coefficient approaches 0.5, it mirrors the characteristics of a step function.

In conclusion, companies that disclose specifics about the damages they have incurred tend to have fewer pronounced stock price reactions. This suggests that investors value this extra detail, as it diminishes ambiguity.

Hypothesis 4 proposes that the depth and detail of damage information affect stock price reactions. Announcements that went beyond

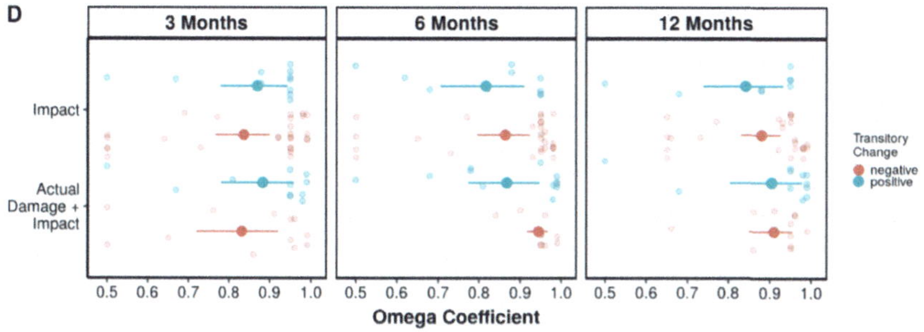

Fig. 2.22 Comparison of impact with impact and actual damage in terms of the omega coefficient

mere impact descriptions and delved into comprehensive damage details led to notable stock price reactions in roughly 10% of instances. What stands out is that a majority of these reactions were positive. On the other hand, announcements that provided only a cursory overview of the impact led to chiefly negative stock price reactions, evident in about 15–20% of cases. This underscores the idea that increased transparency reduces ambiguity—a natural precursor to apprehension. Such clarity can offer investors a better understanding of the extent of the damage and the effectiveness of the company's supply chain management (Filbeck et al., 2016). To conclude, in-depth damage disclosures can diminish the chances of stock price fluctuations, and when fluctuations do occur, they tend to be on the positive side.

2.4.2 *Communication Shapes Market Response*

The study's findings align with previous research highlighting determinants affecting stock price reactions, such as those identified by Dietch and Corey (2011). An unexplored dimension that this research underscores is the profound impact of detailed damage disclosure on stock price outcomes. When companies transparently share in-depth details about damages, particularly from hurricane-related incidents, there are fewer overall stock price shifts.

More importantly, these shifts lean towards being less negative or even positive. This trend suggests that both investors and board members place high value on clarity and transparency, using such information to gauge potential impacts more effectively. Historical data has shown that uncertainty often leads to unpredictable investor responses (Blose et al., 1996).

In practical terms, this research provides actionable insights for boards, communication teams, and supply chain managers. Emphasising transparency in communication, rather than just meeting mandatory disclosure requirements, can stave off negative market repercussions and cultivate greater shareholder trust.

References

Altay, N., & Ramirez, A. (2010). Impact of disasters on firms in different sectors: Implications for supply chains. *Journal of Supply Chain Management, 46*(4), 59–80.

Ariyo, A. A., Adewumi, A. O., & Ayo C. K. (2014). *Stock price prediction using the ARIMA model*. In 2014 UKSim-AMSS 16th international conference on computer modelling and simulation, IEEE, pp. 106–112.

Arrow, K. J. (1970). *Essays in the theory of risk-bearing*. North-Holland.

Beard, E., Marsden, J., Brown, J., Tombor, I., Stapleton, J., Michie, S., & West, R. (2019). Understanding and using time series analyses in addiction research. *Addiction, 114*(10), 1866–1884.

Blackhurst, J., Craighead, C. W., Elkins, D., & Handfield, R. B. (2005). An empirically derived agenda of critical research issues for managing supply-chain disruptions. *International Journal of Production Research, 43*(19), 4067–4081.

Blose, L. E., Bornkamp, R., Brier, M., Brown, K., & Frederick, J. (1996). Catastrophic events, contagion, and stock market efficiency: The case of the space shuttle challenger. *Review of Financial Economics, 5*(2), 117–129.

Boin, A., & McConnell, A. (2007). Preparing for critical infrastructure breakdowns: The limits of crisis management and the need for resilience. *Journal of Contingencies and Crisis Management, 15*(1), 50–59.

Box, G. E., & Tiao, G. C. (1975). Intervention analysis with applications to economic and environmental problems. *Journal of the American Statistical Association, 70*(349), 70–79.

Brooks, R. M., Patel, A., & Su, T. (2003). How the equity market responds to unanticipated events. *The Journal of Business, 76*(1), 109–133.

Caporale, G. M., & Makarenko, I. (2019). Force majeure events and stock market reactions in Ukraine. *Investment Management & Financial Innovations, 16*(1), 334.

Cho, V. (2001). Tourism forecasting and its relationship with leading economic indicators. *Journal of Hospitality & Tourism Research, 25*(4), 399–420.

Chung, R. C., Ip, W., & Chan, S. L. (2009). An ARIMA-intervention analysis model for the financial crisis in China's manufacturing industry. *International Journal of Engineering Business Management, 1*, 5.

Corey, C. M., & Deitch, E. A. (2011). Factors affecting business recovery immediately after hurricane Katrina. *Journal of Contingencies and Crisis Management, 19*(3), 169–181.

De Bondt, W. F., & Thaler, R. H. (1990). Do security analysts overreact? *The American Economic Review, 80*, 52–57.

De Bondt, W. P. (1993). Betting on trends: Intuitive forecasts of financial risk and return. *International Journal of Forecasting, 9*(3), 355–371.

Dietch, E. A., & Corey, C. M. (2011). Predicting long-term business recovery four years after hurricane Katrina. *Management Research Review, 34*(3), 311–324.

Donadelli, M., & Lucchetta, M. (2013). Emerging stock premia: Some evidence from industrial stock market data. *Asian Economic and Financial Review, 3*(4), 398.

Ellis, S. C., Shockley, J., & Henry, R. M. (2011). Making sense of supply disruption risk research: A conceptual framework grounded in enactment theory. *Journal of Supply Chain Management, 47*(2), 65–96.

Fama, E. F., Fisher, L., Jensen, M. C., & Roll, R. (1969). The adjustment of stock prices to new information. *International Economic Review, 10*(1), 1–21.

Filbeck, G., Kumar, S., Liu, J., & Zhao, X. (2016). Supply chain finance and financial contagion from disruptions-evidence from the automobile industry. *International Journal of Physical Distribution & Logistics Management, 46*(4).

Gangopadhyay, P., Haley, J. D., & Zhang, L. (2010). An examination of share price behavior surrounding the 2005 hurricanes Katrina and Rita. *Journal of Insurance Issues, 33*, 132–151.

Helfenstein, U. (1991). The use of transfer function models, intervention analysis and related time series methods in epidemiology. *International Journal of Epidemiology, 20*(3), 808–815.

Hendricks, K. B., & Singhal, V. R. (2003). The effect of supply chain glitches on shareholder wealth. *Journal of Operations Management, 21*(5), 501–522.

Hendricks, K. B., & Singhal, V. R. (2005). Association between supply chain glitches and operating performance. *Management Science, 51*(5), 695–711.

Hendricks, K. B., & Singhal, V. R. (2005). An empirical analysis of the effect of supply chain disruptions on long-run stock price performance and equity risk of the firm. *Production and Operations Management, 14*(1), 35–52.

Hendricks, K. B., & Singhal, V. R. (2008). The effect of supply chain disruptions on shareholder value. *Total Quality Management, 19*(7–8), 777–791.

Hobbs, J., Schaupp, L. C., & Gingrich, J. (2016). Terrorism, militarism, and stock returns. *Journal of Financial Crime, 23*(1), 70–86.

Horwich, G. (2000). Economic lessons of the Kobe earthquake. *Economic Development and Cultural Change, 48*(3), 521–542.

Hyndman, R. J., & Athanasopoulos, G. (2018). *Forecasting: Principles and practice*. OTexts.

Kahneman, D., & Tversky, A. (1973). On the psychology of prediction. *Psychological Review, 80*(4), 237.

Kahneman, D., & Tversky, A. (1979). Prospect theory: An analysis of decision under risk. *Econometrica, 47*(2), 263–291. http://www.jstor.org/stable/1914185

Kaplanski, G., & Levy, H. (2010). Sentiment and stock prices: The case of aviation disasters. *Journal of Financial Economics, 95*(2), 174–201.

Khan, O., & Burnes, B. (2007). Risk and supply chain management: Creating a research agenda. *The International Journal of Logistics Management, 18*(2), 197–216.

Kim, J. M., Son, K., & Kim, Y. J. (2019). Assessing regional typhoon risk of disaster management by clustering typhoon paths. *Environment, Development and Sustainability, 21*, 2083–2096.

Lagarde, M. (2012). How to do (or not to do)… assessing the impact of a policy change with routine longitudinal data. *Health Policy and Planning, 27*(1), 76–83.

López-de Lacalle, J. (2016). *tsoutliers R package for detection of outliers in time series*. CRAN, R Package 95.

Miao, Q., Hou, Y., & Abrigo, M. (2018). Measuring the financial shocks of natural disasters: A panel study of US states. *National Tax Journal, 71*(1), 11–44.

Papadakis, I. S. (2003). On the sensitivity of configure-to-order supply chains for personal computers after component market disruptions. *International Journal of Physical Distribution & Logistics Management, 33*(10), 934–950.

Papadakis, I. S. (2006). Financial performance of supply chains after disruptions: An event study. *Supply Chain Management: An International Journal, 11*(1), 25–33.

Rao, S., & Goldsby, T. J. (2009). Supply chain risks: A review and typology. *The International Journal of Logistics Management, 20*(1), 97–123.

Sheffi, Y., & Rice, J. B., Jr. (2005). A supply chain view of the resilient enterprise. *MIT Sloan Management Review, 47*(1), 41–48.

Tang, C. S. (2006). Robust strategies for mitigating supply chain disruptions. *International Journal of Logistics: Research and Applications, 9*(1), 33–45.

Tan, W. J., & Enderwick, P. (2006). Managing threats in the global era: The impact and response to SARS. *Thunderbird International Business Review, 48*(4), 515–536.

Wagner, S. M., & Bode, C. (2008). An empirical examination of supply chain performance along several dimensions of risk. *Journal of Business Logistics, 29*(1), 307–325.

Wagner, S. M., & Neshat, N. (2012). A comparison of supply chain vulnerability indices for different categories of firms. *International Journal of Production Research, 50*(11), 2877–2891.

Wahdan, M. A., Emam, M. A., et al. (2017). The impact of supply chain management on financial performance and responsibility accounting: Agribusiness case from egypt. *Accounting and Finance Research, 6*(2), 136–149.

Wieland, A., & Wallenburg, C. M. (2012). Dealing with supply chain risks: Linking risk management practices and strategies to performance. *International Journal of Physical Distribution & Logistics Management, 42*(10), 887–905.

Worthington, A., & Valadkhani, A. (2005). Catastrophic shocks and capital markets: A comparative analysis by disaster and sector. *Global Economic Review, 34*(3), 331–344.

Zsidisin, G. A., Petkova, B. N., & Dam, L. (2016). Examining the influence of supply chain glitches on shareholder wealth: Does the reason matter? *International Journal of Production Research, 54*(1), 69–82.

Zsidisin, G. A., & Wagner, S. M. (2010). Do perceptions become reality? The moderating role of supply chain resiliency on disruption occurrence. *Journal of Business Logistics, 31*(2), 1–20.

CHAPTER 3

Hurricane Incident Announcements Across Sectors

Abstract This chapter examines how stock price reactions to hurricane-induced disruptions vary across different industrial sectors. By analysing NYSE-listed firms with significant physical supply chains, the study reveals that while all sectors experience impacts from hurricanes, the magnitude and nature of these effects differ significantly. Sectors such as basic industries, capital goods, and consumer non-durables exhibit the most pronounced negative stock price reactions, highlighting their vulnerability to supply chain disruptions. Conversely, sectors like healthcare and consumer durables often see positive effects, driven by increased demand post-disaster. These findings underscore the importance of sector-specific risk management strategies and the critical role of transparent communication in mitigating negative market responses.

Keywords Hurricane Impact · Stock Price · Industrial Sectors · Supply Chain Disruption · Risk Management · Basic Industries · Capital Goods · Consumer Durables · Investor Reaction · Market Response

This chapter presents research results in terms of variation in stock price reactions to disruptions based on industrial sectors. Existing research evaluates several characteristics of the firm for their potential influence on

P. Schelp et al., *Supply Chain Disruptions and Stock Prices*, Palgrave Studies in Logistics and Supply Chain Management,
https://doi.org/10.1007/978-3-031-68885-0_3

stock prices after disasters and supply chain disruptions such as industry. The effect on market sector returns after disasters differ depending on the industry (Worthington & Valadkhani, 2005).

In the context of supply chain research, this book focuses on NYSE-listed firms with a significant physical supply chain integral to their core business and strategic objectives. For instance, banks procuring basic office supplies or energy providers solely distributing energy are excluded, as are airlines with minimal supply chain involvement. Specific industrial sectors were also excluded for better comparability. Companies were assessed based on inclusion and exclusion criteria, with data collected on stock exchange details, tickers, and industrial sectors for evaluation.

3.1 Hurricane Incidents Affect All Sectors

An initial analysis suggests that some sectors face heightened vulnerability to hurricane occurrences. Companies across all sectors have recorded up to three or four disaster incidents. Narrowing down to just hurricane events, every sector has documented incidents, with several companies noting up to three such events within the span of five years. Remarkably, firms in the consumer durables and basic industry sectors have reported as many as four hurricane incidents.

Figure 3.1 depicts the frequency of natural disasters, including hurricanes, affecting various industrial sectors. On the *y*-axis, distinct industrial sectors are enumerated, while the *x*-axis provides the absolute count of firms. Coloured bar graphs per sector indicate the tally of reported incidents for each company.

Breaking it down further, basic industries (31%), capital goods (17%), consumer non-durables (14%), healthcare (12%), consumer durables (12%), and consumer services (8%) together constitute 94% of the total disaster occurrences.

Announcements on hurricane incidents are made in all industrial sectors, with up to three hurricane incidents announced between 2014 and 2018. Consumer durables and basic industries even had firms reporting up to four hurricane incidents during that time frame. As in previous research, some industrial sectors report more hurricane incidents than others. The most hurricane incident announcing sectors are basic industries, capital goods, healthcare, and consumer non-durables (in that order). Basic industries often use minerals, compounds, and chemicals

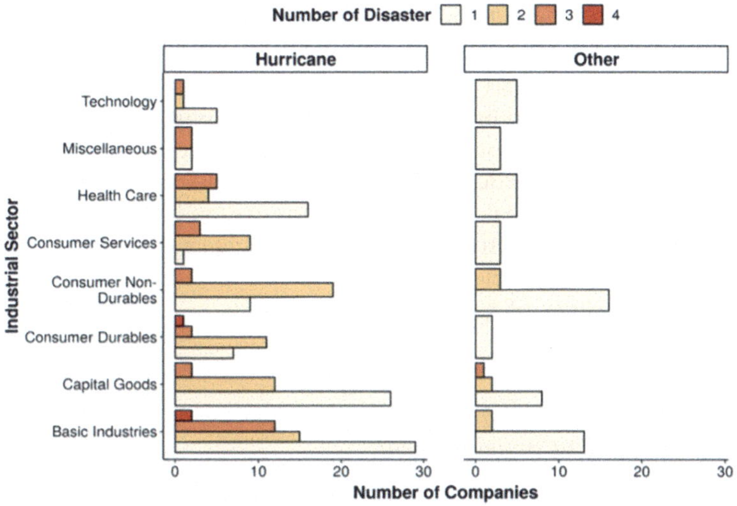

Fig. 3.1 Number of companies per sector announcing the number of their hurricanes and other natural disaster incidents

potentially hazardous to people and the environment and have stricter regulatory requirements, leading to more announcements.

Capital goods tend to be high-value goods with technically complex production, increasing the disruption risk for these firms (e.g., car manufacturers and defence contractors).

Consumer non-durables might lose their (often) perishable goods during such an event. Food has high hygiene requirements. On the other hand, consumer durables often report supply chain disruptions, higher production costs, or decreases in demand.

Many firms in the healthcare sector are based in Puerto Rico and Texas and thus suffered supply chain disruptions due to the hurricanes there.

Agricultural companies are more exposed to natural disasters because most assets, such as fields, are almost impossible to protect from severe weather-related phenomena, i.e., hurricanes. Additionally, similarly to basic industries and capital goods, some companies in other sectors may use hazardous chemicals or produce technically complex devices, which makes them potentially vulnerable to flooding and wind damage. Hurricane incidents might also lead to secondary damage, usually in the form of safety threats to the environment or people. Chemical companies, for example, are exposed to a bigger physical and reputational threat and face tighter regulations to ensure safety.

The descriptive analysis reveals that the frequency of firms making hurricane incident announcements varies depending on the industry. Additionally, the proportion of significant reactions to hurricane incident announcements and hurricane announcements differs across industrial sectors. Moreover, the balance between positive and negative reactions varies distinctly among sectors. These findings suggest that investors make distinctions among industries and hold varying expectations regarding the frequency and severity of specific industry impacts.

H5: *The industrial sector influences the stock price response to a hurricane incident announcement.*

Hypothesis 5 pertains to Anchor A of hurricane incident announcements. It is there to assess the impact of the industrial sector.

The influence of disasters on market sector returns has varied in financial economics literature (Worthington & Valadkhani, 2005). In supply chain management research, the industrial sector was not found to significantly affect the impact of supply chain disruptions on stock price returns; firms across all industrial sectors demonstrated a response (Hendricks & Singhal, 2003; Liu et al., 2018). However, several studies have detected statistically significant differences.

According to one study, consumer services, financial services, and materials sectors are particularly sensitive to disasters (Worthington & Valadkhani, 2005). Another study suggests that the service industry's response is unclear but may remain stable (Webb et al., 2000). Research has also indicated that some industries are more resilient to disasters, with a few even benefiting from them (Dietch & Corey, 2011). Sectors such as construction and manufacturing, essential for reconstruction efforts have been identified as experiencing a positive effect (Zhang et al., 2009). Additionally, a study found that healthcare and utilities sectors exhibited higher stock excess returns following a disaster (Donadelli & Lucchetta, 2013). Given the varying outcomes in previous research, this thesis explores the likelihood and patterns of damage within each industrial sector.

The outcome of the intervention analysis is sorted by industry, providing a breakdown of the number of statistically significant LRTs for each sector across varying time horizons. Two key points emerge: First, there are consistent disruptions within the time series and second, every examined industrial sector experienced significant interruptions.

Three months post-incident, the percentage of companies with significant disruption in their time series spans from 20% to 57%. The technology sector stands out with over 50% of its firms affected. However, this sector consists of fewer than 10 firms, potentially compromising the robustness of this finding. Other sectors such as consumer services (50%), basic industries (36%), consumer durables (30%), and capital goods (29%) also demonstrate disruptions. Even in sectors like consumer durables (23%) and healthcare (19%), a sizable portion of firms is impacted.

The sectors were defined based on their NYSE classification. When the observation window is stretched to either 6 or 12 months, all sectors continue to display interruptions. For some sectors, the extended time frame diminishes the significant reactions of firms by 10–20%. However, basic industries and consumer durables only depict minor variations based on the time frame, hinting at a long-lasting impact (step change).

Figure 3.2 visualises the LRTs by industrial sector. For every firm and hurricane incident announcement pairing, the ARIMA-intervention model with the smallest AIC is taken into account. If the LRT's *p*-value, which contrasts a model without intervention against one with intervention, is under 0.05, the disruption is deemed statistically significant (highlighted in orange). The percentages represent the ratio of significant LRTs for each bar, and both significant and non-significant LRTs are graphed for every industry.

Figure 3.3 presents a breakdown of the most suitable transfer functions, taking into account significant interruptions over different time

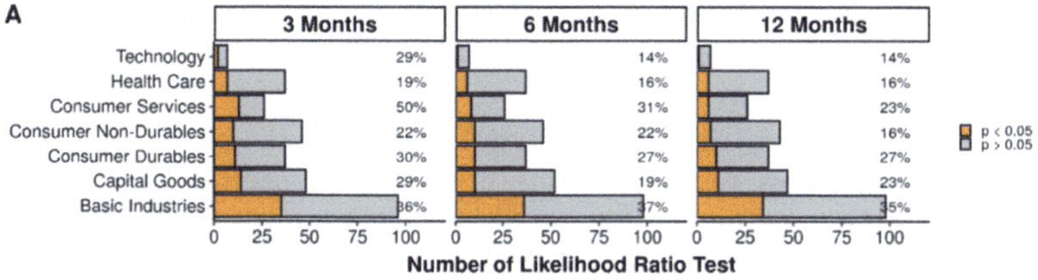

Fig. 3.2 The effects observed across sectors over time

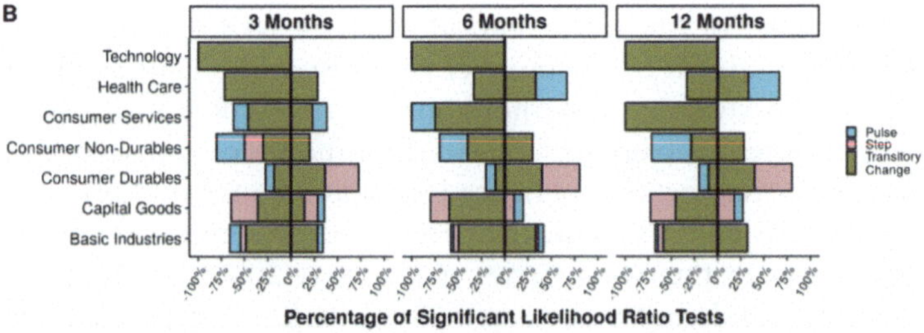

Fig. 3.3 The effects across sectors over time by transfer function

spans for each industry. The direction of change is indicated by a negative LRT. Both upward and downward shifts in stock prices are observed. Crucially, both the magnitude and the direction of these changes are consistent regardless of the duration post-incident. Basic industries, in particular, display a mix of short-lived positive and negative changes. Consumer services and capital goods, predominantly exhibiting short-term fluctuations, lean towards more negative stock price variations.

In Fig. 3.3, the transfer functions and their directionality are depicted for each firm type in relation to hurricane incident announcements. Each sector's bars, segmented by time horizon, total 100%. The graphic shows the distribution of the three most fitting transfer functions—step (in rose), short-lived change (in olive), and pulse (in light blue)—for each industry, based on the proportion of significant LRTs that align best with each function. The left side of the 0 line showcases negative reactions, while the right side highlights positive ones.

Figure 3.4 illustrates the extent of effect change in percentage terms. There are only limited coefficient estimates available for each transfer function, as can be observed from the minimal statistically significant LRTs per sector in Fig. 3.3. This can lead to significant, or sometimes non-determinable, standard errors. However, when changes do manifest, their magnitude appears to be consistent, irrespective of whether they are positive or negative.

Figure 3.4 depicts the effect alterations for step, pulse, and transitory functions across the three time horizons for each industry sector. Effects to the left of the zero line indicate negative transfer function coefficients (represented by circles), while those to the right denote positive coefficients (symbolised by triangles).

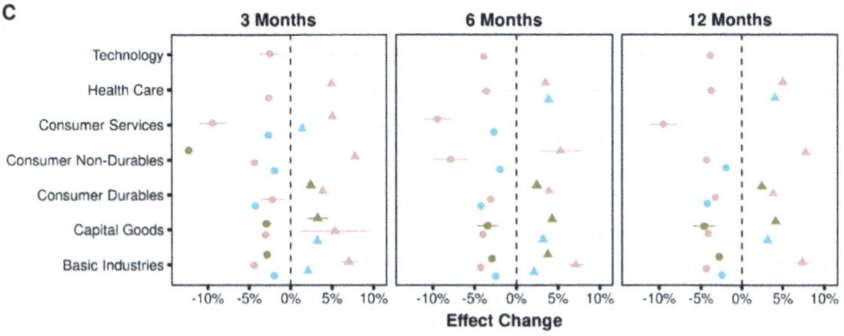

Fig. 3.4 The effect change across sectors over time

Figure 3.5 displays the omega coefficient for the transitory change transfer functions across three time horizons for each sector. As the omega coefficient approaches 1.0, the effect diminishes more rapidly, resembling a pulse function. Conversely, when the omega coefficient is closer to 0.5, it aligns more with a step function.

The proportion of significant reactions to hurricane incident announcements and hurricane announcements differs across industrial sectors. Moreover, the balance between positive and negative reactions varies distinctly among sectors. These findings suggest that investors make distinctions among industries and hold varying expectations regarding the frequency and severity of specific industry impacts.

The influence of industrial sectors is confirmed. Significant reactions to hurricane incident announcements vary between industrial sectors, aligning with previous research (Worthington & Valadkhani, 2005). We

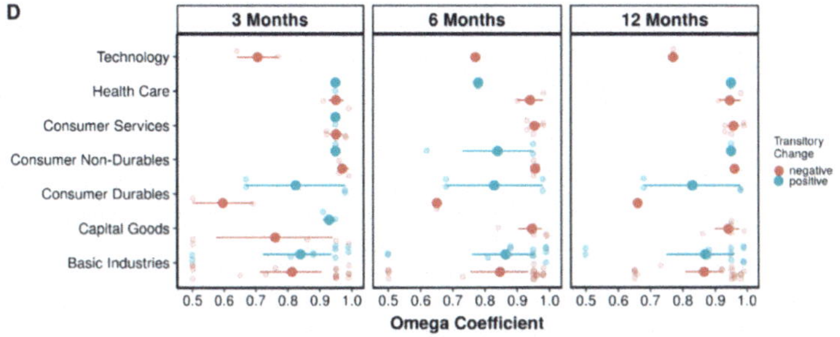

Fig. 3.5 The Omega coefficient across sectors over time

used the NYSE industrial sector classification for the main analysis we found that all industrial sectors were affected, consistent with prior studies (Hendricks & Singhal, 2003; Liu et al., 2018).

In the consumer non-durables sector, there were noticeable reactions, but they normalised quickly, suggesting short-term concerns about product losses and facility hygiene. High-value equipment suppliers faced negative reactions due to the sensitivity of their products. On the other hand, some apparel companies reported positive reactions.

The capital goods sector exhibited a 30% interruption rate over three months, indicating concerns over high-value inventory destruction. Consumer Durable firms experienced a step change in stock prices, possibly due to increased demand post-hurricane.

Results for the technology and healthcare sectors were inconclusive due to the limited number of companies.

Overall, industrial sectors influence stock price reactions, with basic industries and capital goods showing the highest proportion of significant and negative reactions. Consumer services and consumer non-durables also had negative reactions but with lower overall significance.

In summary, the study highlights the impact of industrial sectors on stock price reactions to hurricane incidents, demonstrating variations in both the frequency and nature of these reactions across sectors.

3.2 Implications for Risk Management

This study reaffirms prior research findings that stock price effects follow hurricane incident announcements across all sectors as per Hendricks and Singhal (2003). However, the extent and direction of these effects vary by industry, echoing the differentials highlighted in earlier studies (Worthington & Valadkhani, 2005). Predominantly, sectors like consumer services, non-durables, capital goods, and basic industries experience adverse effects. This contrasts with the healthcare and consumer durables sectors, which generally show more favourable outcomes due to increased post-disaster demands.

The pronounced negative effect in the capital goods sector is a novel observation. One contributing factor might be that previous studies didn't classify "capital goods" as a distinct category or the particular sensitivity of capital goods to disaster-specific supply chain disruptions given the potential for extensive damage to high-value assets in this industry.

From a supply chain risk management standpoint, different patterns emerge across sectors. For instance, capital goods and consumer non-durables witness lasting negative reactions, implying the need for heightened SCRM. In contrast, healthcare and consumer durables generally have positive effects, possibly because of a surge in demand post-disaster. This surge in demand might be considered by investors as a sustainable benefit, especially in the aftermath of hurricanes.

In terms of actionable insights for businesses, understanding the industry-specific nuances of stock price reactions is crucial. This comprehension allows companies to anticipate stock price fluctuations and strategies accordingly. For sectors like capital goods, safeguarding expensive assets and possibly considering preemptive measures like early facility closures become paramount. For sectors like consumer non-durables, swift supply chain recovery to ensure product availability becomes essential.

In summary, while all sectors are affected by post-hurricane announcements, the nature and magnitude of the stock price reactions vary, urging businesses to tailor their risk management strategies accordingly. Firms of all sectors show a stock price reaction after a hurricane incident announcement, and most of these reactions are negative. However, the reactions differ, meaning-specific preparation is required depending on the company's sector. Two sectors showed more positive reactions, i.e., the healthcare and the durables sector, meaning that these have to be the least concerned. Companies from the sectors of consumer non-durables, capital goods, and basic industries, and consumers themselves, are highly likely to have a negative stock price effect, indicating that these companies especially need to proactively manage hurricane risk.

Another insight is that the proportions of best-fitting patterns are industry-specific—even though overall, the best-fitting pattern is the transitory function. This shows that, depending on the industry, investors have different expectations of how lasting the damage is. A high proportion of pulse functions indicate investors tend to express a quick shock (overreaction), which does not necessarily require management response. However, a high proportion of step functions indicate a sustained stock price reaction and show that investors expect severe longer-term damage. Capital goods companies and consumer non-durables especially show negative step functions.

Capital goods companies are investment intense; companies from this sector need to demonstrate that they have a solid supply chain risk management framework and that they do everything to protect their expensive assets—possibly with early voluntary closures.

Consumer non-durables live from shelf availability. Their supply chain risk management needs to focus on making sure that they can recover their supply chain quickly in order to make their products available to the customer as soon as possible. Given the industry of a company, management can anticipate the extent, directionality, and pattern of reaction. The results were stable throughout the time horizons, apart from noticeable changes in the healthcare sector.

Firms need to communicate in a transparent manner to reduce shareholders' uncertainty and build trust. When a firm announces hurricane incident announcements, providing details on the damage makes any stock price reaction less likely. On top of negative reactions being less likely, positive reactions are relatively more likely. It seems that the provided information reduces uncertainty for the boards and stockholders as they can anticipate the effect by receiving more information. Not only that, but the results also provide the boards, communication departments, and supply chain managers with the depth of information the market appreciates. Firms that are providing just the necessary, i.e., mandatory, information are punished by shareholders because the less information they have, the higher their uncertainty. Firms in all sectors are affected; however, the effects vary between industries.

References

Dietch, E. A., & Corey, C. M. (2011). Predicting long-term business recovery four years after Hurricane Katrina. *Management Research Review, 34*(3), 311–324.

Donadelli, M., & Lucchetta, M. (2013). Emerging stock premia: Some evidence from industrial stock market data. *Asian Economic and Financial Review, 3*(4), 398.

Hendricks, K. B., & Singhal, V. R. (2003). The effect of supply chain glitches on shareholder wealth. *Journal of Operations Management, 21*(5), 501–522.

Liu, J., Sarkar, S., Kumar, S., & Jin, Z. (2018). An analysis of stock market impact from supply chain disruptions in Japan. *International Journal of Productivity and Performance Management, 67*(1), 192–206.

Webb, G. R., Tierney, K. J., & Dahlhamer, J. M. (2000). Businesses and disasters: Empirical patterns and unanswered questions. *Natural Hazards Review, 1*(2), 83–90.

Worthington, A., & Valadkhani, A. (2005). Catastrophic shocks and capital markets: A comparative analysis by disaster and sector. *Global Economic Review, 34*(3), 331–344.

Zhang, Y., Lindell, M. K., & Prater, C. S. (2009). Vulnerability of community businesses to environmental disasters. *Disasters, 33*(1), 38–57.

CHAPTER 4

Preventive Closures to Mitigate Hurricane Impacts

Abstract This chapter investigates the impact of preventive closures, implemented by governments or companies in anticipation of hurricanes, on stock prices. By analysing historical data and reporting behaviours, the study reveals that proactive supply chain risk management, including preventive closures, often stabilises stock prices in the face of hurricane threats. These closures, whether government-mandated or voluntary, are viewed favourably by shareholders, who recognise their role in minimising long-term damage and preserving business continuity. The findings highlight the importance of transparency and proactive measures in building investor confidence and ensuring operational resilience in hurricane-prone regions.

Keywords Preventive Closures · Hurricane Impact · Stock Price · Supply Chain Risk Management · Business Continuity · Investor Confidence · Operational Resilience · Proactive Measures · Disaster Preparedness · Transparency

This chapter explains closure decisions taken by governments or companies as a preventive measure after a hurricane prediction and their effect on stock prices. By examining past hurricane incidents and reporting

P. Schelp et al., *Supply Chain Disruptions and Stock Prices*, Palgrave Studies in Logistics and Supply Chain Management,
https://doi.org/10.1007/978-3-031-68885-0_4

behaviours, this chapter provides valuable insights into the importance of proactive supply chain risk management.

In the face of impending natural disasters, such as hurricanes, governments, and companies alike are forced to make critical decisions to protect their assets, employees, and surrounding communities. One of the key strategies employed in this context is preventive closures. This chapter delves into the rationale and consequences of these preventive closures, particularly with regard to their impact on stock prices.

Preventive closures encompass a range of actions taken to mitigate the potential harm caused by hurricanes. While homeowners may simply install shutters, more comprehensive measures are required for the protection of entire communities. For companies, the decision to close facilities may be influenced by various factors (Dietch & Corey, 2011; Sebastian et al., 2017).

In the face of major disasters, both government entities and businesses proactively adopt measures to mitigate the potential impact of hurricanes. Individual companies often find it necessary to close their own facilities, either in response to government-issued preventive mandates or as a voluntary component of their supply chain strategy. Firms typically close, for example, their production facilities due to concerns about the vulnerability of their structures during normal operations or the potential for operational activities to pose risks to the environment, workforce, or neighbouring facilities, e.g., Sebastian et al. (2017). Firms also can be severely affected by company or infrastructure way up their supply chain.

Government measures can vary in scope, from individual homeowners adding protective shutters to safeguard their private residences https://disastersafety.org to more extensive efforts involving flood prevention and the closure of critical infrastructure to protect entire communities. During hurricanes, critical infrastructure elements, including communication networks, roads, rails, shipping terminals, and airports, are often temporarily closed to mitigate potential damage (Sebastian et al., 2017). The decision regarding which infrastructure to close lies outside a company's control. Consequently, businesses must adapt their supply chain strategies accordingly if they are still operational during such events. Preventive closures are not a one-size-fits-all approach.

4.1 Preventive Closure and Supply Chain-Related Facilities

The data analysis reveals that preventive closures of supply chain-relevant facilities, including production and storage facilities, can result in supply chain disruptions. These closures may be regulated by guidelines or mandated by law, but many companies choose to act proactively to safeguard their assets and employees (Ellis et al., 2011).

Supply chain disruptions, as a result of hurricane-induced damage or closures, can have far-reaching consequences for companies. It's not just about the immediate financial impact; it's also about reputational damage and long-term business continuity. Companies that prioritise preventive closures as part of their supply chain risk management strategies tend to fare better in the face of natural disasters (Sheffi & Rice Jr, 2005).

4.2 Preventive Closures of Infrastructure

In contrast to company-specific facilities, preventive closures of infrastructure, such as airports, ports, and railways, are typically ordered by the government. These closures are often part of broader evacuation plans announced by the government for disaster-affected regions. Due to their government-issued nature, companies may not disclose these closures explicitly. Government-mandated infrastructure closures play a crucial role in ensuring public safety during hurricane events. These closures, often part of coordinated disaster response plans, are intended to minimise the risk to individuals and the disruption to essential services. For example, during Hurricane Irma in 2017, airports in Florida were closed well in advance of the storm's landfall to prevent accidents and ensure the safety of passengers and airport staff.

Although preventive closures may temporarily disrupt operations, shareholders may appreciate them for their potential to reduce or prevent more severe damage in the long run (Papadakis, 2006; Wagner & Neshat, 2012). Therefore, preventive closures can be seen as an active supply chain strategy or supply chain risk management measure. They can take many forms, including the shutdown of production facilities, evacuation orders, and the closure of critical infrastructure. To understand the intricacies of preventive closures, let's delve deeper into the various aspects of this multifaceted strategy.

For example, Hurricane Katrina in 2005 wreaked havoc on the Gulf Coast of the United States. In its aftermath, numerous reports documented the extensive damage caused to oil refineries and chemical plants. Preventive closures of these facilities, even though disruptive at the time, were instrumental in preventing catastrophic environmental disasters and long-term supply chain disruptions (McGee, 2008).

This research explores whether providing specific information on preventive closures of production facilities affects the stock price effect when a hurricane incident is announced. To test this hypothesis, researchers have analysed historical stock price data in the aftermath of hurricane incidents. The results suggest that companies that implement preventive closures tend to experience less severe stock price fluctuations in response to hurricane announcements compared to those that do not take such measures.

4.3 Reporting Behaviour of Companies

Companies' reporting behaviour during hurricane incidents varies. Some firms report only on the impact without providing details on preventive closures or supply chain-related damage. Others go a step further by disclosing information about preventive measures and the damage incurred. Firms that experience an impact from a hurricane incident are more likely to report on preventive closures as part of their risk management strategy.

Transparency in reporting is crucial for maintaining investor confidence and managing expectations (Firth et al., 2015). Investors rely on accurate and timely information to assess the potential financial impact of hurricane events on companies' operations and profitability. Companies that provide comprehensive reports, including details on preventive measures, tend to enjoy more stable stock prices in the wake of hurricanes.

In the energy sector, previous research showed that hurricanes had little impact on the stock returns of companies (Liu et al., 2021). Even though the impact is small, the stocks of oil, natural gas, nuclear and renewable energy companies generally performed better than those in the coal industry following hurricanes. In conclusion, hurricanes provide information about firms' future profitability based on their carbon intensity.

4.4 The Impact of Preventive Closures

Preventive measures against climate risks and routine improvements in resilience can stabilise and boost investor confidence in the face of extreme climate change shocks and their negative impacts, thereby smoothing out abnormal stock price fluctuations caused by climate disasters (Gao et al., 2024). Preventive closures essentially serve as a form of insurance against the financial fallout of hurricanes. While they may entail short-term costs, such as facility shutdowns and supply chain disruptions, the long-term benefits in terms of operational continuity and reputation preservation are substantial. Investors, recognising this, tend to view companies that implement preventive closures favourably. As the frequency and severity of climate disasters increase, it is necessary to understand individual preparedness and risk-reduction activities (Mol et al., 2020).

Detailed reporting on preventive closures reassures shareholders that companies are taking responsible and prudent measures to protect their assets and ensure business continuity. This transparency builds trust and may even enhance a company's long-term stock performance.

4.5 Encouraging Proactive Measures

The results indicate that firms providing such information are unlikely to experience significant positive or negative stock price effects, suggesting that shareholders appreciate proactive supply chain risk management (Child, 1972; Dietch & Corey, 2011).

Finally, the chapter highlights that shareholders tend to support preventive measures, even if they result in temporary supply chain disruptions. Preventive closures, whether government-ordered or voluntary, are seen as prudent actions to prevent more severe damage. This encourages supply chain managers to adopt preventive measures and promotes transparency in sharing this information with the public.

The positive response of shareholders to proactive supply chain risk management strategies, including preventive closures, underscores the importance of taking a long-term view of disaster preparedness. While the immediate costs and disruptions may be significant, the potential long-term benefits, both in terms of financial stability and reputational resilience, make preventive closures a wise choice for companies operating in hurricane-prone regions. An integrated assessment is necessary to identify sustainable solutions to reduce climate-related risks with input from a range of disciplines (Andersson-Sköld et al., 2015).

4.6 Conclusion

Providing information on preventive closures to protect equipment and staff rarely leads to a reaction or a negative reaction. The results suggest that shareholders seem to support preventive measures if government inflicted—and then it applies to all firms or if self-chosen by a firm.

The support of shareholders even applies if these lead to a temporary supply chain disruption as a means to safeguard long-term operations and minimise further disruptions. Even if a firm chooses a voluntary closure of production facilities, investors prefer a minor disruption over the increased risk of the firm suffering a large disruption due to the hurricane hitting the firm when fully operational. Often, companies that prioritise and transparently report on preventive closures tend to enjoy more stable stock prices in the aftermath of hurricanes.

In essence, preventive closures serve as a proactive form of insurance that protects both financial interests and reputations, ultimately contributing to a company's long-term resilience in the face of natural disasters. This encourages supply chain managers to take preventive measures, even when these lead to a temporary disadvantage, to prevent worse damage, as well as encouraging boards and senior management to condone these preventive measures and share that information with the public rather than hiding it. In conclusion, preventive closures of facilities typically do not result in negative stock price effects.

References

Andersson-Sköld, Y., Thorsson, S., Rayner, D., Lindberg, F., Janhäll, S., Jonsson, A., Moback, U., Bergman, R., & Granberg, M. (2015). An integrated method for assessing climate-related risks and adaptation alternatives in urban areas. *Climate Risk Management, 7*, 31–50.

Child, J. (1972). Organizational structure, environment and performance: The role of strategic choice. *Sociology, 6*(1), 1–22.

Dietch, E. A., & Corey, C. M. (2011). Predicting long-term business recovery four years after hurricane katrina. *Management Research Review, 34*(3), 311–324.

Ellis, S. C., Shockley, J., & Henry, R. M. (2011). Making sense of supply disruption risk research: A conceptual framework grounded in enactment theory. *Journal of Supply Chain Management, 47*(2), 65–96.

Firth, M., Wang, K., & Wong, S. M. (2015). Corporate transparency and the impact of investor sentiment on stock prices. *Management Science, 61*(7), 1630–1647.

Gao, X., Dong, S., Liu, C., & Wang, H. (2024). Proactive green innovation and firm climate resilience: The nonlinear interaction effect of climate risk. *Environmental Science and Pollution Research*, 1–30.

Liu, H., Ferreira, S., & Karali, B. (2021). Hurricanes as news? Assessing the impact of hurricanes on the stock market returns of energy companies. *International Journal of Disaster Risk Reduction, 66*, 102572.

McGee, R. W. (2008). An economic and ethical analysis of the katrina disaster. *International Journal of Social Economics, 35*(7), 546–557.

Mol, J. M., Botzen, W. W., & Blasch, J. E. (2020). Risk reduction in compulsory disaster insurance: Experimental evidence on moral hazard and financial incentives. *Journal of Behavioral and Experimental Economics, 84*, 101500.

Papadakis, I. S. (2006). Financial performance of supply chains after disruptions: An event study. *Supply Chain Management: An International Journal, 11*(1), 25–33.

Sebastian, T., Lendering, K., Kothuis, B., Brand, N., Jonkman, B., van Gelder, P., Godfroij, M., Kolen, B., Comes, T., Lhermitte, S., & Meesters, K. (2017). *Hurricane harvey report: A fact-finding effort in the direct aftermath of hurricane harvey in the greater houston region.*

Sheffi, Y., & Rice, J. B., Jr. (2005). A supply chain view of the resilient enterprise. *MIT Sloan Management Review, 47*(1), 41–48.

Wagner, S. M., & Neshat, N. (2012). A comparison of supply chain vulnerability indices for different categories of firms. *International Journal of Production Research, 50*(11), 2877–2891.

CHAPTER 5

Incident Announcements vs. Hurricane Announcements

Abstract This chapter examines the differential impacts of general hurricane announcements and specific incident announcements on stock prices. By analyzing NYSE-listed firms, the study reveals that both types of announcements can significantly affect stock prices, often triggering negative reactions. The research highlights that even the anticipation of a hurricane, independent of direct impact, can influence investor behaviour. Furthermore, the study introduces a novel comparison between hurricane incident and general hurricane announcements, employing transfer functions to identify patterns of stock price reactions, predominantly observing transitory changes indicative of overreactions. These findings underscore the critical importance of timely and transparent communication in mitigating adverse stock market responses.

Keywords Hurricane Announcements · Incident Announcements · Stock Price Reaction · Supply Chain Disruption · Efficient Market Hypothesis · Investor Behavior · Risk Communication · Contagion Effect · Overreaction · Transfer Functions

P. Schelp et al., *Supply Chain Disruptions and Stock Prices*, Palgrave Studies in Logistics and Supply Chain Management,
https://doi.org/10.1007/978-3-031-68885-0_5

This chapter distinguishes general announcements about hurricanes from specific incident announcements. It explains how stock prices react to different types of announcements.

Figure 5.1 represents the approaches employed for the dual scenarios under review. For the initial scenario, the pivotal moment is the disclosure of the hurricane incident. This approach is exclusively viable for companies that reported hurricane incidents from 2014 to 2018. Yahoo Finance's API provides the necessary NYSE stock price data for each firm. This data also offers insights into industrial sectors and company announcements in response to hurricanes.

In the secondary scenario, we introduce distinct "Anchor B" as benchmarks for analysis. These benchmarks provide a comprehensive overview, encompassing all firms, irrespective of whether they made announcements. This offers a nuanced comparative study between announcers and non-announcers.

Just like in the primary scenario, Yahoo Finance's API facilitates the evaluation of the impact of hurricane announcements on stock prices based on NYSE stock data. However, due to data granularity leading to potential computational challenges, we do not test the impact of industry sectors or impact type. For a fair comparison, we considered only those hurricane incident announcements made after the hurricane's inception.

Figure 5.1 can be split into two segments: The top part deals with the methodology for hurricane incident disclosures (termed "Anchor 1"), while the bottom portion explores general hurricane alerts (dubbed "Anchor 2"). Both segments detail data origins, data pathways, involved variables, targeted hypotheses, and anticipated results.

5.1 Announcements of Hurricane Incidents vs. General Hurricane Alerts

The likelihood of a supply chain disruption originating from a disaster event is generally low. However, when such an event occurs, it can lead to significant costs (Horwich, 2000). The efficient market hypothesis posits that in an efficient market, any new information, including the announcement of a supply chain disruption, is rapidly incorporated into the stock price (Fama et al., 1969; Hendricks & Singhal, 2003; Najam & Mehmood, 2019).

Previous research has provided empirical support for this theory, with studies showing a 10% decline in stock prices for listed companies

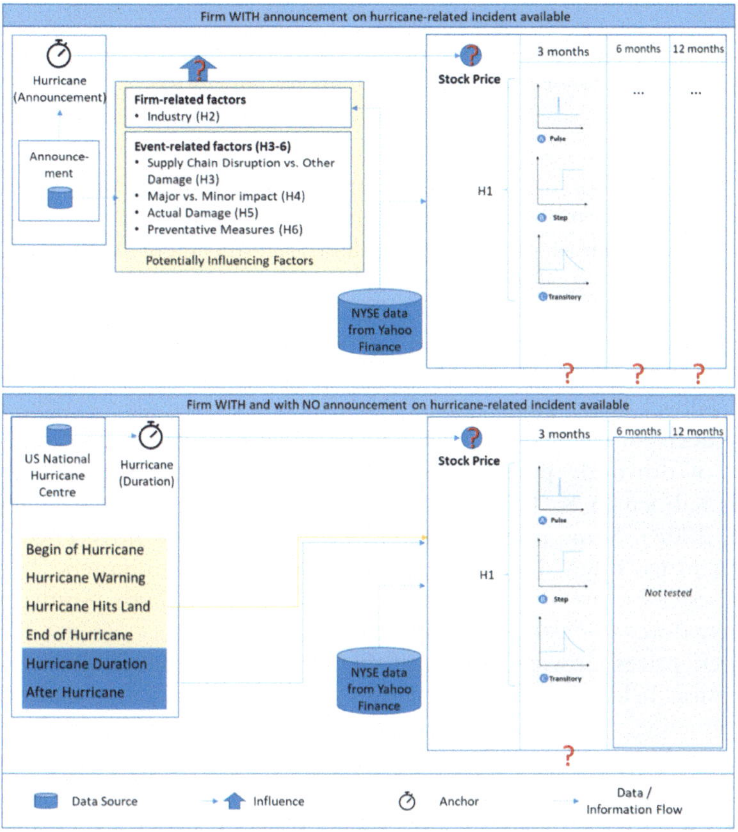

Fig. 5.1 Testing for the two anchors

following supply chain disruption announcements (Hendricks & Singhal, 2003, 2008). More recent studies confirm a noticeable but less substantial decrease in stock price returns (Zsidisin et al., 2016). Supply chain disruptions resulting from natural disasters, such as earthquakes, have been linked to significant Cumulative Abnormal Returns (Papadakis, 2006).

The impact of force majeure events, particularly natural disasters, has been observed to have an immediate and substantial adverse effect on stock price returns on the first trading day (Caporale & Makarenko, 2019). Based on these observations, Hypothesis H1 is formulated.

Hypothesis 1 (H1): *The announcement of a hurricane incident/ hurricane announcement has an impact on stock prices.*

Our study examines not only firm-specific announcements but also general hurricane announcements to enable a comparison of investor reactions to risk (such as a hurricane incident announcement) with reactions to uncertainty (e.g., hurricane landfall). This approach is supported by the contagion theory, which describes how market reactions can spread to companies in the same industry or location, as evidenced by changes in their stock prices, even if they are not directly affected by the event itself (Filbeck et al., 2016).

In decision theory and finance, risk is considered not only in terms of downside potential but also the upside possibilities (Arrow, 1970; Kahneman & Tversky, 1979; Rao & Goldsby, 2009; Wagner & Bode, 2008). Some previous studies have identified positive effects on certain firms, often due to increased demand during disasters. In our hypothesis, we use the term "effect" to encompass both positive and negative outcomes associated with risk.

Stock prices provide a quantifiable measure of the subjective risk perception held by shareholders, thus allowing us to gauge and translate this subjective risk into an objective risk perspective (Khan & Burnes, 2007; Zsidisin & Wagner, 2010). The subjective perception of investors is reflected in the objective measurement of stock prices, often manifesting in specific patterns. Therefore, identifying different patterns is crucial for reverse-engineering the source of subjective risk perception. For example, investors react differently to anticipated and unanticipated disasters, with slower reactions to unanticipated events, likely because they need time to form opinions on subjective risks. Hurricanes can be considered somewhat anticipated, but their unpredictable path and uncertain impact make it interesting to study how investors react to different hurricane-related information or impact assessments.

Stock price reactions following a disruption, such as a hurricane, can be analysed using transfer functions represented as pulse, step, and transitory change functions of time series data (Box & Tiao, 1975). Specific stock price patterns can also serve as indicators of psychological phenomena. For instance, a pulse pattern aligns with the overreaction hypothesis, suggesting that investors and security analysts tend to overreact to both positive and negative news, resulting in unjustified stock price reactions (De Bondt, 1993; De Bondt & Thaler, 1990; Filbeck et al., 2016).

Research supports this overreaction, showing a significant negative reaction on the day of and the day after a supply chain disruption announcement (Filbeck et al., 2016; Hendricks & Singhal, 2003). Additionally, a significant long-term decrease in stock price returns has been observed in the year following an SCD (Hendricks & Singhal, 2005). Although a consistent negative relationship between supply chain disruptions/disasters and stock price returns has been established, the magnitude and duration of these effects vary (Hendricks & Singhal, 2003; Zsidisin et al., 2016).

Therefore, Hypothesis 1 is divided into three sub-hypotheses to examine the nature of stock price reactions.
Hypothesis 1a (H1a): *A hurricane incident announcement/ hurricane announcement has a short-term impact on stock prices, characterised by a pulse function.*
Hypothesis 1b (H1b): *A hurricane incident announcement/ hurricane announcement has a lasting impact on stock prices, represented as a step function.*
Hypothesis 1c (H1c): *A hurricane incident announcement/ hurricane announcement has a temporary impact on stock prices, defined as a transitory change function.*

5.2 Description and Collection of Hurricane Announcement Data

The data on the hurricane announcements are collected from the National Hurricane Centre. In the archive, a yearly overview of all tropical cyclones, namely hurricanes, storms, and tropical depressions, is provided. The annual Tropical Cyclone Advisory Archive is divided into Atlantic, East Pacific, and Central Pacific regions. An "Advisory Archive" for each hurricane is sorted into different columns according to the advisory type. As this book aims to evaluate the reaction to publicly available data, the column "public advisories" is selected. The public advisories are sorted by date and time and provide a link to a hurricane report.

A tropical cyclone is the term used independently of wind speed; they do not tend to be classified as hurricanes right from the beginning but build up over time until they reach hurricane strength with wind speeds above 74 miles per hour. Updates on tropical cyclones with wind speeds up to 74 miles per hour are provided every 5–6 hours. Once 74 miles per hour are exceeded, immediate reports are published between the regular reports. All reports per hurricane are reviewed.

Data are extracted from each report and collected in a database; data related to all hurricanes in the predefined time frame of five years from 2014 to 2018 are collected. However, due to data processing restrictions, only the eight hurricanes mentioned in incident announcements by firms were selected for modelling.

From the detailed information in the individual reports on the eight hurricanes, the parameters are selected that are most likely to have an impact on stock price, namely the following four specific points in time and two time frames:

1. **Begin of Hurricane (Point in Time):** The first time a tropical cyclone is called a hurricane. In this case, the heading of the report changes to, e.g., "Hurricane Florence Intermediate Advisory Number 51A". There is not necessarily information about if and when the hurricane will hit land; it is solely information on the strength of the tropical cyclone.
2. **Hurricane Warning (Point in Time):** A hurricane warning is always launched in connection with a geographical link. It means that a particular area is threatened by a hurricane. The definition of a hurricane warning in a report may look like this: "A Hurricane Warning means that hurricane conditions are expected somewhere within the warning area. A warning is typically issued 36 hours before tropical storm-force winds' anticipated occurrence, conditions that make outside preparations difficult or dangerous. Preparations to protect life and property should be rushed to completion". This definition of a hurricane warning is an example from Hurricane Florence in 2018. The time frame given in the reports varies slightly. The example of the warning itself is: "A Hurricane Warning is in effect for...* South Santee River South Carolina to Duck North Carolina * Albemarle and Pamlico Sounds". This information was

also selected as an example from the report "Hurricane Florence Intermediate Advisory Number 51A".

3. **Hurricane Landfall (Point in Time):** If a hurricane hits land, there will be a report just after or at the time the hurricane hits land. The report will comprise the time and location of landfall and the possible path.
4. **End of Hurricane (Point in Time):** The end of the hurricane is marked by the first report that does not classify the tropical cyclone as a hurricane anymore but as a tropical storm or depression.
5. **Hurricane Duration (Time frame):** The hurricane duration is the time between the above-defined points of time the hurricane begins and the end of the hurricane.
6. **After Hurricane (Time frame):** The three months after the above-defined end of the hurricane.

5.3 Anchors

An anchor serves as the point of interruption, also referred to as intervention in ITSA. This thesis examines two anchors.

5.3.1 Anchor A: Hurricane Incident Announcement

Figure 5.2 illustrates that Anchor A marks the interruption of the time series, set on the date of the initial public announcement containing information about the hurricane incident related to a specific firm. This analysis assesses whether the anchor time, defined by the announcement day, can be identified as a significant outlier in the time series. The anchor corresponds to the announcement date; however, if the announcement date falls on a non-trading day, the next trading day is selected.

5.3.2 Anchor B: Hurricane Announcement

Anchor B encompasses announcements related to a particular hurricane but not specifically linked to a particular firm. It includes several anchor points:

Begin of Hurricane (Point in Time): The start of the hurricane is chosen as the first anchor point. Although this information primarily indicates the strength of the tropical cyclone and does not yet signify a threat

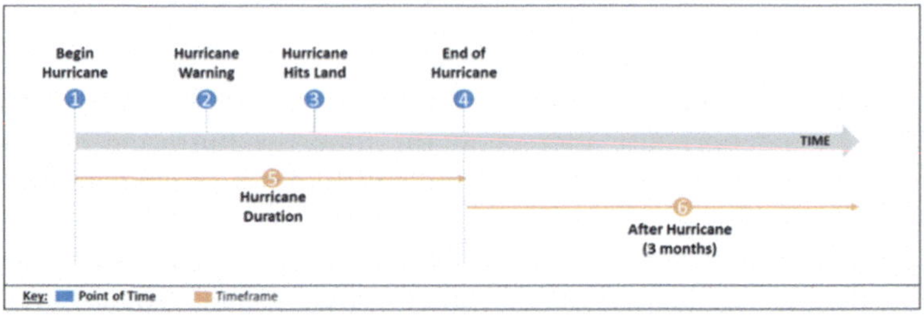

Fig. 5.2 Type B hurricane announcement anchors

to land, it can trigger reactions from people who may respond negatively due to the potential hurricane threat.

Hurricane Warning (Point in Time): The hurricane warning is selected as the second anchor because it connects the hurricane to a specific landfall. Preceding a hurricane warning, there are often hurricane watches (indicating the possibility of a hurricane), but hurricane warnings carry more significance (warning to prepare for a hurricane). This information signals a tangible hurricane threat to a specific geographical area, and negative reactions from people are expected, likely reflected in stock prices.

Hurricane Landfall (Point in Time): The announcement that a hurricane has made landfall represents the first indication of a 100% likelihood of impact. People are expected to react negatively to the realisation of a disaster.

End of Hurricane (Point in Time): People may respond differently to this information. Some might react positively, relieved that the hurricane has subsided, while others may react negatively due to the damage caused by the hurricane.

Hurricane Duration (Time frame): To analyse effects during the duration of the hurricane, the hurricane's total duration is selected. It is predicted that people will react negatively while the hurricane is ongoing.

After Hurricane (Time frame): Initially, time frames of 3, 6, and 9 months were examined. However, as the results were very similar, a 3-month time frame was ultimately applied. This period allows for the assessment of reactions following the hurricane's conclusion.

5.4 H1: General Hurricane-Related Information

In the subsequent part of our analysis, we utilise various hurricane announcement dates as anchors to model their impact on stock prices, including:

1. The beginning of the hurricane.
2. Hurricane warning.
3. Hurricane landfall.
4. The conclusion of the hurricane.
5. The duration of the hurricane.
6. The aftermath of the hurricane.

For each hurricane, we conduct tests on the stock price development of both announcing and non-announcing firms. We identify the most suitable pattern to characterise their reactions. For Anchors B1–4, which represent specific points in time, we employ the pulse and transitory change functions. Conversely, for Anchors B5–6, which represent time intervals, the step function is utilised.

For all eligible companies, we consider all eight hurricanes with their Anchor B defined. Figure 5.3 provides an overview of the intervention analysis concerning the responses of both announcing and non-announcing firms after Anchor B.

Figure 5.3 illustrates the reactions of both announcing and non-announcing firms following Anchor B. If the p-value from the Likelihood Ratio Test (LRT) comparing a null model (absence of intervention) with the intervention model falls below the nominal threshold of 0.05, the modelled interruption is deemed statistically significant, indicated by the orange colour.

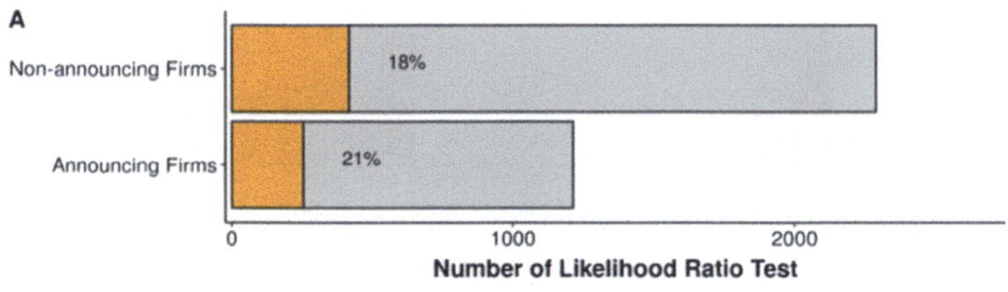

Fig. 5.3 Reaction of announcing and non-announcing firms after Anchor B

The percentage displayed represents the proportion of LRTs that are statistically significant for each bar. The results indicate that approximately 21% of the reactions among announcing firms are statistically significant. For non-announcing firms, this figure is slightly lower, at around 18%. This suggests that both announcing and non-announcing firms exhibit statistically significant stock price reactions to hurricane-related information, with approximately 20% of each group demonstrating such reactions.

Figure 5.4 provides a more detailed breakdown of the Likelihood Ratio Test results, presenting the LRT outcomes for each of the six Anchor B types concerning the reactions of both announcing and non-announcing firms. Among announcing firms, the anchors "begin of hurricane" and "hurricane warning" yield the highest proportion of statistically significant reactions, each at 23%, followed by "hurricane hitting land" (21%), "end of hurricane", and "after the hurricane" (20% each). In contrast, "hurricane duration" exhibits significance in only 10% of the cases, showing a notable difference from the other anchors.

For non-announcing firms, the LRT results per anchor are more closely aligned. "Hurricane warning" leads with the highest LRT at 22%, closely followed by "hurricane hitting land" (20%), "hurricane duration" (18%), "end of hurricane" and "after the hurricane" (17% each), and "begin of

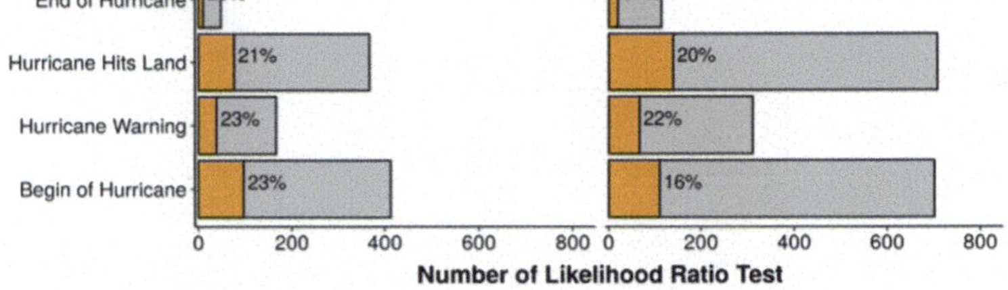

Fig. 5.4 Reaction by points in time and time frames

hurricane" with 16%. All tested anchors result in a proportion of statistically significant reactions, indicating that shareholders take note of and respond to all hurricane-related information.

Figure 5.4 displays the outcomes of the ARIMA-Intervention Model for Hurricane Weather Forecasting (Part I), showing the number of Likelihood Ratio Tests (LRTs) for each Firm Type and Weather Forecast Anchor. We consider the ARIMA-intervention model with the lowest AIC for each firm and hurricane. If the p-value from the LRT comparing a null model (absence of intervention) with the intervention model falls below the nominal threshold of 0.05, the modelled interruption is considered statistically significant, denoted by the orange colour. The percentage displayed represents the proportion of statistically significant LRTs for each bar. There is only one endpoint for each hurricane, but for some hurricanes, there are multiple starting points and warnings.

Figure 5.5 provides an overview of the relative proportions of transfer functions associated with each anchor. For both announcing and non-announcing firms, each anchor defines an interruption represented by a specific function. For Anchors B 1–4, which correspond to points in time, pulse, and transitory functions are applied. The step function is applied for Anchors B 5–6, which represent intervals.

Overall, the reactions of both announcing and non-announcing firms tend to be more negative. Comparatively, announcing firms exhibit more negative reactions than non-announcing firms across all anchor

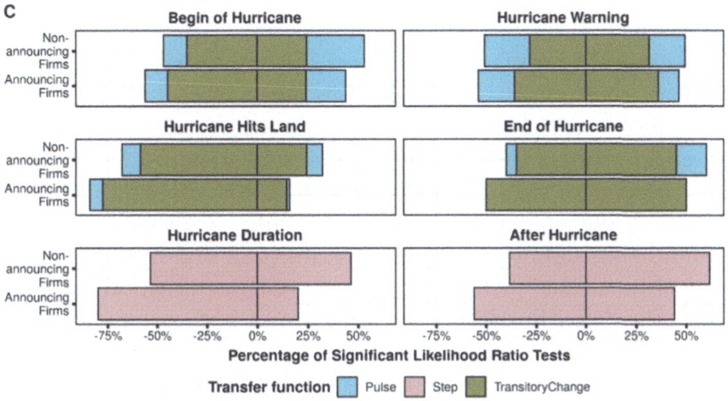

Fig. 5.5 Reaction by transfer function

categories. Notably, for the first four anchors (beginning of hurricane, hurricane warning, hurricane landfall, and end of hurricane), the transitory change function results in a greater degree of negative significance when compared to the pulse function. The highest proportion of negative reactions occurs when a hurricane makes landfall, and this holds true for all firms and functions. A similar proportion of negative reactions is observed only for the hurricane duration among announcing firms.

Figure 5.5 presents the outcomes of the ARIMA-Intervention Model for Hurricane Weather Forecasting (Part I), highlighting the directionality of interruptions for each Firm Type and Weather Forecast Anchor. Each bar represents 100%, and a negative percentage indicates that a portion of the bar exhibits a statistically significant Likelihood Ratio Test (LRT) with a negative coefficient for the estimated effect. The colour reflects the best-fitting transfer function for the model with a statistically significant LRT and the lowest AIC for the specific firm, hurricane, and weather forecast anchor. Please note that for each hurricane, there is only one endpoint, although some hurricanes may have multiple starting points and warnings.

We observe that, while less frequent, there were more negative reactions associated with the "beginning of hurricane" anchor when using the transitory function for all firms. Conversely, for non-announcing firms, there was a higher proportion of positive reactions compared to negative reactions at the "end of the hurricane" and "after the hurricane" anchors. For the first four anchors, the transitory function was the best fit for the majority of cases. Additionally, for the "beginning of hurricane" and "hurricane warning" anchors, the pulse function was the best fit in approximately 15–20% of cases.

The magnitude of effect changes for the transitory change function, expressed as a percentage, is illustrated in Fig. 5.6.

In Fig. 5.6, when changes occurred, the magnitudes of negative and positive effect changes were generally quite similar, with a few exceptions. Notably, there were strong negative reactions for non-announcing firms at the "beginning of hurricane" with the pulse function, as well as for both announcing and non-announcing firms (to a slightly lesser extent) at the "end of hurricane" when the transitory change function was applied. Moreover, the "after hurricane" anchor showed both strong negative and positive reactions for non-announcing firms.

Figure 5.6 depicts the outcomes of the ARIMA-Intervention Model for Hurricane Weather Forecasting (Part II), specifically illustrating the effect changes per Firm Type and Weather Forecast Anchor. For each

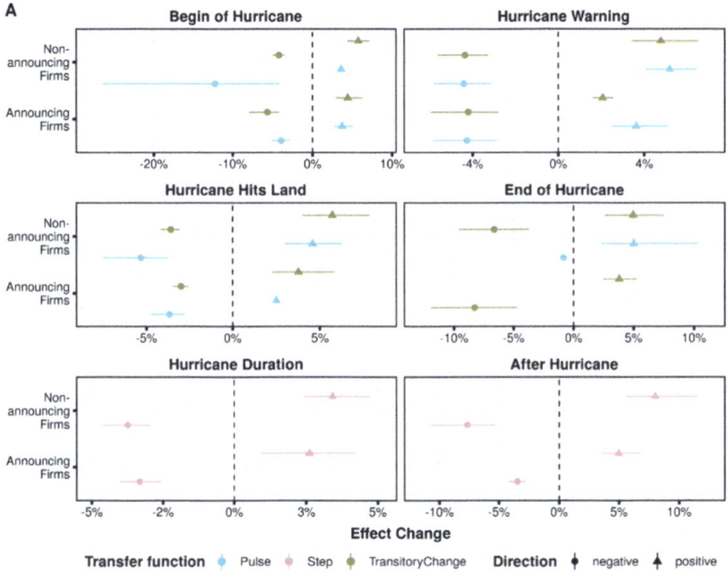

Fig. 5.6 Reaction by effect change

combination of firm and hurricane, we selected the ARIMA-intervention model with the lowest AIC and a statistically significant LRT, which compared the null model (no intervention) to the intervention defined by the anchor. The coefficient of the transfer function was then converted into an estimated percentage difference in stock price at the anchor point. For the transitory change function, we calculated the median effect over the first four days following the anchor point.

Figure 5.7 provides an overview of the omega coefficient associated with the transitory change function. In almost all cases, the omega coefficient closely approximates 1.0. This suggests that both positive and negative effects diminish rather rapidly. The most rapid decay is observed for the "end of hurricane" anchor function, with one notable exception—the positive reaction of non-announcing firms, which exhibits a relatively slower decay.

The results presented in Fig. 5.7 stem from the ARIMA-Intervention Model for Hurricane Weather Forecasting (Part II). Specifically, the figure illustrates the Omega Coefficient per Firm Type and Weather Forecast

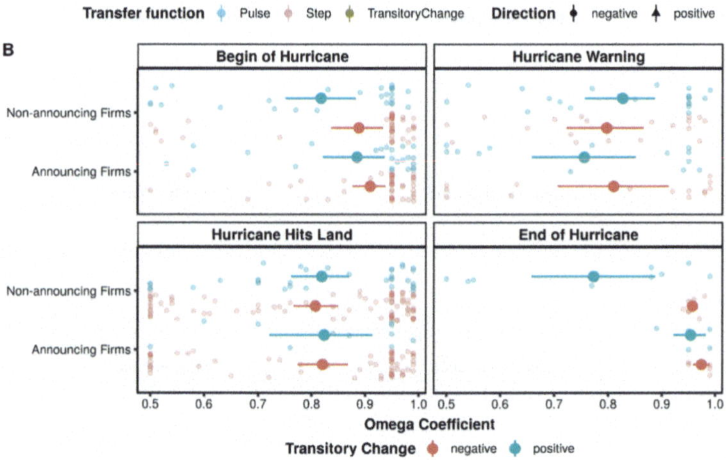

Fig. 5.7 Reaction by omega coefficient

Anchor. For each combination of firm and hurricane, we selected the ARIMA-intervention model with the lowest AIC and a statistically significant LRT, comparing the null model (no intervention) to the model with intervention defined by the anchor. If the identified model utilises the transitory change function as the transfer function, the corresponding omega coefficient, which determines the rate of gradual increase (depicted in green for the positive direction) or decrease (depicted in red for the negative direction), is displayed. Additionally, the figure includes the mean estimated omega coefficient (+/− std. error) per firm type and weather forecast anchor, presented in corresponding bold colours.

Different anchor points are determined to identify the most relevant and compare the effect of general hurricane-related news or information with actual hurricane incident announcements on firms. The anchor point "hurricane incident announcement" is tested in a time series outlier analysis. Outliers are detected in 87% of the time series, which indicates the suitability of Anchor A as an interruption of the time series. Hurricane announcements, as well as hurricane incident announcements, cause a reaction in stock prices (H1). Hurricane-related information and hurricane incident-related firm announcements are shown to have a significant effect on firm performance in 25–31% of cases. Most of these stock price effects tend to be negative.

5.5 Discussion and Contributions

Before delving into the primary analysis, an outlier analysis of the time series was conducted to validate the selection of hurricane incident announcements as appropriate anchor points in the main model. In this study, the announcement dates were subjected to a statistical assessment to ascertain their suitability as anchor points. The results of this analysis showed that interruptions in the time series were identified in 87% of the companies within the scope of the study. Moreover, it was found that the majority of these interruptions, which corresponded to the announcement of hurricane incidents, were indeed detectable and significant disruptions. This empirical evidence firmly establishes that announcements made by firms regarding hurricane incidents serve as suitable and meaningful anchor points in the analysis.

The discussion follows a structured approach based on the hypotheses. We begin by analysing Hypothesis 1, including its sub-hypotheses, using both types of anchors to model their respective effects on stock prices for each firm: hurricane incident announcements and hurricane announcements. To identify significant changes in stock prices, we employ the most appropriate pattern, whether it's a pulse, transitory change, or step, for various time horizons, spanning 3, 6, and 12 months after the anchor point.

Hypothesis 1 states that hurricane incident announcements and hurricane announcements have a significant effect on stock price, which is in alignment with the efficient market hypothesis (Kahneman & Tversky, 1973). Stock price allows the measurement of the subjective risk perceived by the shareholders in order to translate it into an objective risk view (Khan & Burnes, 2007; Zsidisin & Wagner, 2010). The reaction patterns defined in the sub-hypotheses to H1 allow for estimating subjective and objective components.

For Hurricane Incident Announcements, H1 was tested positive as around 30% of the announcing firms show a significant interruption associated with the announcement day in the time series. This finding is in line with the efficient market hypothesis and is supported by findings from previous research.

Event studies showed statistically significant reactions after announcements of supply chain disruptions and disasters (Caporale & Makarenko, 2019; Hendricks & Singhal, 2003, 2008; Zsidisin et al., 2016). These results are more specific and specifically show company announcements' effects on hurricane incidents. Additionally, the results show that these interruptions are quite stable even when extending the time period from three to six or twelve months. Aligned with previous research findings, there are more negative than positive extreme values (Hendricks & Singhal, 2003, 2008).

In this research, it was detected that many of the extreme values occurred when hurricane damage from two directly consecutive hurricanes was announced—mostly hurricanes Harvey and Irma; the companies were CMG, AXE, CLW, VRTV, CSS, and FTK. This happens because hurricane incident announcements are mostly made at the end of the hurricane season, often aggregating reports of multiple hurricane incidents.

Overall, the results of the intervention analysis provide insight that the transitory change function fits best in most cases (more than 60%). Even for the extreme values, this is true with just one exception: ATI. As expected, the overall stock price reaction of firms was more negative (Hendricks & Singhal, 2003). Hurricanes cause a lot of destruction, e.g., Hurricane Harvey alone costing the US economy 125 billion USD (National Hurricane Center, https://www.nhc.noaa.gov).

The transitory change function indicates that there might be a component of overreaction in stock price—if the function approximates a pulse pattern. The absence of a pulse pattern indicates that the reaction is not solely an overreaction (Filbeck et al., 2016). The more abundant negative stock price effects disappear faster than the few positive reactions. The faster fading of negative effects may be due to hurricane damages being repaired and investors forgetting the incident over time. In conclusion, hurricane incidents are most likely to cause a strong negative sudden stock price reaction that fades over time, which is supported by previous research findings.

For Hurricane Announcements, H1 tested positive for around 21% of the reactions of announcing firms and for 18% of the non-announcing firms. As announcements are tied to the hurricanes but not to the companies, it seems that investors, based on their intuition and/or past experience, can partially anticipate which companies will be suffering damage.

Different hurricane information was tested in the form of different anchors: the beginning of a hurricane, hurricane warning, hurricane hits land, end of a hurricane, hurricane duration, and after the hurricane. All tested anchors led to a proportion of statistically significant reactions, indicating that all hurricane information is noted and reacted upon by shareholders. For announcing and non-announcing firms, the highest percentage of statistically significant reactions (23%) was found. This is in alignment with the efficient market hypothesis that investors react immediately to newly available information (Kahneman & Tversky, 1973).

Even though the earliest information tested was "the beginning of a hurricane",—this information means that the storm has reached a certain speed, but it still might be somewhere on the ocean, far away from land. In contrast, the next point of time "hurricane warning" is tied to a location and it is the first time an imminent threat is quite certain; however, the extent of its damage is uncertain and therefore leads to overreactions (Filbeck et al., 2016).

5.5.1 Comparing Hurricane Incident Announcements with General Hurricane Information

In this section, we delve into a novel comparison by analysing the effects of hurricane incident announcements against the backdrop of general hurricane announcements. Specifically, we focus on the impact observed at the time of hurricane landfall (anchor B3), where stockholders react to the realisation that a hurricane threat has materialised. Investor reactions are influenced by their expectations regarding whether a company will be affected and the severity of that impact.

For announcing firms, we observe a significant proportion of reactions across all anchor points (Anchor Bs), underscoring investors' ability to anticipate potential damage. Concerning points in time, the transitory function stands out as the most suitable function for the majority of the data, marked by high omega coefficients. This indicates strong but rapidly fading reactions, suggestive of an overreaction component (Filbeck et al., 2016). The duration of the hurricane introduces uncertainty for investors, as firms require time to assess the impact (Filbeck et al., 2016). This uncertainty is reflected in the substantial negative reactions observed for announcing firms in the form of a step function. The prolonged negative impact might be attributed to investors having to grapple with uncertainty until firms release pertinent information, often in subsequent quarterly or annual reports.

Investors also respond to information conveyed through the announcement of a hurricane incident at the time of the announcement itself (Anchor A). Intriguingly, the transitory change function appears to be the most appropriate, signifying an overreaction component to the announcement, coupled with a longer-lasting effect. In the case of hurricane incident announcements, investors appear to reward companies that furnish detailed information while penalising those that merely comply with the minimal regulatory requirements. The closer alignment between the results of the analyses for Anchors A and B suggests that investors were better at anticipating the impact on the firm. A strong correlation is evident between the outcomes for both anchors.

Moreover, distinct industrial sectors exhibit varying frequencies, directions, and magnitudes of reactions, highlighting diverse investor responses across sectors. Industries such as non-durables, basic industries, and capital goods tend to experience the most negative reactions. Investors might exhibit more prolonged negative reactions when faced with potential impact (e.g., hurricane duration) due to the dearth of information, in contrast to their response to negative news where the impact is known (e.g., the announcement of hurricane impact as an anchor). The provision of detailed information and preventive measures notably mitigates the intensity of investor reactions.

5.5.2 Research Insights

Hurricane-related announcements, whether concerning incidents or mere predictions, significantly influence stock prices, often negatively. This trend aligns with previous studies showing the adverse effects of disasters and supply chain disruptions on stock prices. Supporting the efficient market hypothesis, the market reacts promptly to such announcements, reflecting the information's incorporation into stock prices.

A novel comparison introduced by this study is between hurricane incident announcements and general hurricane announcements. It emerged that even before direct effects or damage announcements, firms' stock prices respond to general hurricane information, indicating investor sensitivity to uncertainty and possible contagion effects.

Another innovation of this study was employing transfer functions to discern stock price reaction patterns. The most common pattern was the transitory change function, indicating a temporary reaction with a potential overreaction spike. This observation was consistent across multiple time horizons, affirming the robustness of the findings.

5.5.3 *Practical Implications*

Given the inevitable nature of disasters, corporate preparedness is paramount. Even the anticipation of a hurricane or its announcement can affect stock prices due to the contagion effect. Thus, effective and timely communication with shareholders is crucial.

Companies must recognise that mere information about a hurricane, coupled with uncertainties surrounding potential damages, can elicit shareholder reactions. The observed transitory stock price effect, characterised by a potential overreaction, underscores the need for proactive communication. Even if unaffected by the hurricane, companies are advised to promptly issue a negative announcement to allay investor concerns, potentially counteracting the overreaction and benefiting the firm in the long run.

Both hurricane incident announcements and hurricane announcements negatively affect a firm's stock price, mostly in the form of a transitory change. A hurricane incident announcement is when hurricane damage to a firm is publicly reported. A hurricane announcement is a public announcement on a hurricane, such as a hurricane warning or hurricane landfall, which is not tied to any firm.

A company does not even need to suffer damage or publish damage to have its stock price affected due to contagion effects. A firm's stock price may be affected if a hurricane or hurricane landfall is predicted or announced. Just the information on a hurricane and the uncertainty regarding potential future damage can induce a shareholder reaction. Investors fear the potential damage. They are hesitant when the hurricane already hits, and little or no information is provided regarding how severe the hurricane's damage is. Therefore, companies need to communicate as soon as possible to their shareholders, providing details of the damage. The stock price effect is mostly described by a transitory function indicating an overreaction component followed by a return to normality over time. To prevent or reduce this overreaction, companies that are not affected are advised to publish a negative announcement to inform their shareholders and stakeholders that the company is not affected, as this will be beneficial.

A firm does not be affected by a hurricane to suffer damage; it is sufficient to be in geographic proximity to a hurricane.

References

Arrow, K. J. (1970). *Essays in the theory of risk-bearing*. Amsterdam: North-Holland.

Box, G. E., & Tiao, G. C. (1975). Intervention analysis with applications to economic and environmental problems. *Journal of the American Statistical Association, 70*(349), 70–79.

Caporale, G. M., & Makarenko, I. (2019). Force majeure events and stock market reactions in Ukraine. *Investment Management & Financial Innovations, 16*(1), 334.

De Bondt, W. F., & Thaler, R. H. (1990). Do security analysts overreact? *The American Economic Review*, 52–57.

De Bondt, W. P. (1993). Betting on trends: Intuitive forecasts of financial risk and return. *International Journal of Forecasting, 9*(3), 355–371.

Fama, E. F., Fisher, L., Jensen, M. C., & Roll, R. (1969). The adjustment of stock prices to new information. *International Economic Review, 10*(1), 1–21.

Filbeck, G., Kumar, S., Liu, J., & Zhao, X. (2016). Supply chain finance and financial contagion from disruptions-evidence from the automobile industry. *International Journal of Physical Distribution & Logistics Management, 46*(4)

Hendricks, K. B., & Singhal, V. R. (2003). The effect of supply chain glitches on shareholder wealth. *Journal of Operations Management, 21*(5), 501–522.

Hendricks, K. B., & Singhal, V. R. (2005). Association between supply chain glitches and operating performance. *Management Science, 51*(5), 695–711.

Hendricks, K. B., & Singhal, V. R. (2008). The effect of supply chain disruptions on shareholder value. *Total Quality Management, 19*(7–8), 777–791.

Horwich, G. (2000). Economic lessons of the Kobe earthquake. *Economic Development and Cultural Change, 48*(3), 521–542.

Kahneman, D., & Tversky, A. (1973). On the psychology of prediction. *Psychological Review, 80*(4), 237.

Kahneman, D., & Tversky, A. (1979). Prospect theory: An analysis of decision under risk. *Econometrica, 47*(2), 263–291. http://www.jstor.org/stable/1914185

Khan, O., & Burnes, B. (2007). Risk and supply chain management: Creating a research agenda. *The International Journal of Logistics Management, 18*(2), 197–216.

Najam, N. U. S, & Mehmood, A. M. (2019). The economic cost of terrorism and natural disasters: A deeper analysis of the financial market markets of Pakistan

Papadakis, I. S. (2006). Financial performance of supply chains after disruptions: An event study. *Supply Chain Management: An International Journal, 11*(1), 25–33.

Rao, S., & Goldsby, T. J. (2009). Supply chain risks: A review and typology. *The International Journal of Logistics Management, 20*(1), 97–123.

Wagner, S. M., & Bode, C. (2008). An empirical examination of supply chain performance along several dimensions of risk. *Journal of Business Logistics, 29*(1), 307–325.

Zsidisin, G. A., & Wagner, S. M. (2010). Do perceptions become reality? The moderating role of supply chain resiliency on disruption occurrence. *Journal of Business Logistics, 31*(2), 1–20.

Zsidisin, G. A., Petkova, B. N., & Dam, L. (2016). Examining the influence of supply chain glitches on shareholder wealth: Does the reason matter? *International Journal of Production Research, 54*(1), 69–82.

CHAPTER 6

Conclusions

Abstract This chapter synthesises the key findings of the study, emphasising the significant impact of hurricane-related events on stock prices and the importance of proactive risk management. The research highlights that hurricane announcements, whether general or specific to incidents, generally trigger negative stock price reactions. It underscores the importance of industry-specific preparation and effective supply chain risk management, with transparency in corporate communication playing a crucial role in mitigating adverse effects. The study contributes to both academic knowledge and practical applications, offering valuable insights for firms in managing hurricane-related risks and preparing for future challenges.

Keywords Hurricane Risk Management · Stock Price Reaction · Supply Chain Disruption · Corporate Communication · Investor Behavior · Proactive Measures · Industry-Specific Preparation · Efficient Market Hypothesis · Disaster Preparedness · Financial Markets

This chapter concludes the book, summarising key takeaways for both practitioners and academics on managing Hurricane-Related Risks based on our research findings. The summary encapsulates the critical outcomes

P. Schelp et al., *Supply Chain Disruptions and Stock Prices*, Palgrave Studies in Logistics and Supply Chain Management,
https://doi.org/10.1007/978-3-031-68885-0_6

of our research, shedding light on the intricate relationship between hurricanes, supply chain disruptions, and firm performance. Our study draws from a diverse range of academic sources, offering profound insights into the imperative of proactive management and transparent communication during hurricane-induced supply chain disruptions.

6.1 Contribution to Knowledge

6.1.1 Hurricane Announcements Lead to Mostly Negative Reactions

Our research reinforces existing studies highlighting the adverse impact of disasters on stock prices (Caporale & Makarenko, 2019; Papadakis, 2006). We introduce a unique perspective by comparing hurricane incident announcements and hurricane announcements, shedding light on investor behaviour and the role of communication in mitigating stock price reactions. Our findings corroborate the efficient market hypothesis (Fama et al., 1969), underscoring the significance of timely information dissemination.

In exploring Hypothesis 1, we confirm that hurricanes and hurricane-related incidents indeed have a substantial impact on stock prices, aligning with the broader body of research recognising the disruptive influence of disasters on financial markets (Caporale & Makarenko, 2019). Moreover, we find that the effect of such announcements is primarily negative, highlighting the rapid reaction of markets to new information (Fama et al., 1969). An intriguing aspect of our study is the distinction between announcing and non-announcing firms as a control group, revealing that stock prices can react even before official announcements, underscoring the role of uncertainty and investor anticipation (Blose et al., 1996).

6.1.2 Industry Moderates Stock Price Reactions

Our research expands our understanding of how various industries respond to hurricane announcements, aligning with prior studies emphasising sector-specific vulnerabilities (Hendricks & Singhal, 2003; Worthington & Valadkhani, 2005). The negative impact on stock prices is not uniform across all sectors. We discover that industries such as consumer services, consumer non-durables, capital goods, and basic industries tend to endure the most negative effects. This underscores the importance of industry-specific preparation and supply chain risk management (Worthington & Valadkhani, 2005).

Furthermore, we delve into industry-specific stock price patterns following hurricane announcements. While the transitory change function prevails across industries, the proportions of other best-fitting patterns differ. For instance, the capital goods sector predominantly exhibits negative reactions and step functions, indicating sustained stock price declines. In contrast, the healthcare and consumer durables sectors often display positive reactions, suggesting resilience to hurricane incidents (Dietch & Corey, 2011; Donadelli & Lucchetta, 2013).

6.1.3 Minor Supply Chain Disruptions Elicit Positive Reactions

Our research distinguishes between major and minor supply chain disruptions and their impact on stock prices. While previous studies have primarily focused on the negative effects of supply chain disruptions, our findings introduce a novel perspective. Major supply chain disruptions indeed lead to predominantly negative stock price reactions, aligning with prior research (Hendricks & Singhal, 2003, 2008; Zsidisin et al., 2016). However, our research uncovers a unique phenomenon—minor supply chain disruptions often result in positive stock price reactions. This novel insight suggests that shareholders value effective supply chain risk management that prevents more severe disruptions (Zsidisin et al., 2016).

Furthermore, our study categorises supply chain disruptions and other damage, providing a comprehensive understanding of their distinct effects. This approach enriches the literature on supply chain disruptions by highlighting the financial implications of different types and severities of disruptions Caporale and Makarenko (2019).

6.1.4 Transparency in Communication Matters

Transparency in corporate communication emerges as a crucial factor in shaping stock price reactions. Our research underscores the significance of providing specific information on damage following hurricane incidents, a factor previously overlooked in the literature (Dietch & Corey, 2011). Shareholders appreciate detailed information, which reduces uncertainty and fosters trust. This aligns with principles of information transparency and its positive impact on investor behaviour (Blose et al., 1996).

Our findings suggest that companies that offer more comprehensive information on the extent of damage experience fewer negative stock price reactions and, in many cases, positive reactions. This indicates that investors value a high level of detail in hurricane incident announcements and penalise a lack of transparency. Managers can leverage this insight to enhance their response to and preparation for hurricane-related events, both in terms of SCRM and corporate communications (Blose et al., 1996).

6.1.5 Proactive Measures Are Supported

Our research explores preventive closures of production facilities during hurricanes, revealing that shareholders support such proactive measures, even when they result in temporary supply chain disruptions (Papadakis, 2006). Companies that choose voluntary closure of production facilities are unlikely to experience negative stock price reactions, highlighting the value of proactive supply chain risk management efforts.

In practice, our findings suggest that companies should not hesitate to implement preventive measures during hurricane threats. The potential benefits of preventing extensive damage and maintaining operational continuity outweigh the short-term disruptions. Companies can communicate these decisions transparently to shareholders, emphasising their commitment to supply chain resilience and risk management.

6.2 Contribution to Practice

6.2.1 Active Management of Hurricane Risks

Our research underscores the proactive management of hurricane-related risks, aligning with the principles of disaster risk reduction. It emphasises the importance of timely communication to mitigate stock price reactions and provides guidance on the nature of communication, including the use of negative announcements.

In practice, our findings serve as a compelling reminder to companies that hurricanes are not "black swan" events but foreseeable risks that require strategic preparation. By actively managing hurricane risks through effective SCRM and transparent communication, companies can better navigate these challenges and minimise their impact on stock performance.

6.2.2 *Sector-Specific Preparation*

Our findings offer practical insights for firms across industries, emphasising the importance of active hurricane risk management. Sector-specific preparations are essential, and our research aids in understanding expected stock price reactions based on industry, guiding strategic decisions. Practically, our research encourages companies to recognise that while hurricanes pose risks to all sectors, tailored preparations are necessary to address sector-specific vulnerabilities. Boards and senior management can use our insights to inform strategic decisions regarding supply chain risk management and disaster preparedness.

6.2.3 *Prioritise Supply Chain Resilience*

Our research encourages firms to prioritise supply chain resilience, especially in the face of major supply chain disruptions (Zsidisin et al., 2016). The positive stock price reactions to effective supply chain risk management underscore the financial benefits of reducing the severity of disruptions. In practice, our findings suggest that companies should allocate resources and efforts toward managing and mitigating supply chain disruptions. Effective supply chain risk management strategies, such as diversifying suppliers, implementing redundancy plans, and improving visibility across the supply chain, can help reduce the financial impact of disruptions.

6.2.4 *Transparent Communication Builds Trust*

Our research highlights the critical role of transparent communication in reducing stock price reactions (Blose et al., 1996). Providing specific information on damage fosters trust and minimises uncertainty, aligning with principles of information transparency. In practice, our findings underscore the importance of clear and detailed communication during hurricane-related incidents. Firms should proactively provide information to shareholders, the media, and the public to ensure that accurate information is disseminated swiftly. This not only reduces uncertainty but also helps maintain the trust of stakeholders.

6.2.5 *Take Proactive Measures*

Our findings encourage firms to proactively implement preventive closures when necessary, aligning with principles of risk reduction (Papadakis, 2006). Shareholders generally support such measures, even when they result in temporary disruptions, as they prevent more severe damage. In practice, our research suggests that companies should not hesitate to implement preventive measures during hurricane threats. The potential benefits of preventing extensive damage and maintaining operational continuity outweigh the short-term disruptions. Companies can communicate these decisions transparently to shareholders, emphasising their commitment to supply chain resilience and risk management.

6.3 Conclusion

In conclusion, our research emphasises the proactive management of hurricane-related risks through effective supply chain risk management and transparent communication. Hurricanes are not "black swan" events but foreseeable risks that require strategic preparation. By applying the insights from this research, companies can enhance their resilience and minimise the impact of hurricanes on their performance, aligning with principles of disaster risk management and corporate governance. These findings not only contribute to the academic literature but also offer practical guidance for companies seeking to navigate the complex landscape of hurricane-related risks and supply chain disruptions.

6.4 Prospects for Future Studies

The horizon for future research in this field is broad and diverse. In the context of hurricanes, studies could delve into the impact of sequential hurricanes or analyse how various hurricane categories and their distinct characteristics influence stock prices. Comparative research is also ripe for exploring how different types of disasters, both historical and contemporary, affect market values. An examination over time could reveal patterns in how stock prices respond to assorted disasters, individually and collectively.

Cross-national studies could investigate how disaster impacts on stock prices vary by the country of the stock's listing. It would be particularly insightful to focus on disasters that have a global reach or, even more pertinently, a single disaster impacting multiple nations. Additionally, establishing and examining different reference points could yield significant findings. Other potential factors that may influence stock prices warrant identification and examination.

One emergent area of interest is the economic influence of the COVID-19 pandemic on businesses worldwide, which presents an opportunity to study the varied responses of global indices and different industry sectors. The effects of statements by political figures updates from relevant organisations like the World Health Organization, or breaking news developments offer further fertile ground for research. Comparing the current pandemic's economic impact with past health crises, such as the Ebola and Swine flu outbreaks, could provide valuable context. Overall, the research methodology employed here holds great promise for uncovering a wealth of nuanced insights into how disasters shape financial markets.

References

Blose, L. E., Bornkamp, R., Brier, M., Brown, K., & Frederick, J. (1996). Catastrophic events, contagion, and stock market efficiency: The case of the space shuttle challenger. *Review of Financial Economics, 5*(2), 117–129.

Caporale, G. M., & Makarenko, I. (2019). Force majeure events and stock market reactions in Ukraine. *Investment Management & Financial Innovations, 16*(1), 334.

Dietch, E. A., & Corey, C. M. (2011). Predicting long-term business recovery four years after hurricane katrina. *Management Research Review, 34*(3), 311–324.

Donadelli, M., & Lucchetta, M. (2013). Emerging stock premia: Some evidence from industrial stock market data. *Asian Economic and Financial Review, 3*(4), 398.

Fama, E. F., Fisher, L., Jensen, M. C., & Roll, R. (1969). The adjustment of stock prices to new information. *International economic review, 10*(1), 1–21.

Hendricks, K. B., & Singhal, V. R. (2003). The effect of supply chain glitches on shareholder wealth. *Journal of Operations Management, 21*(5), 501–522.

Hendricks, K. B., & Singhal, V. R. (2008). The effect of supply chain disruptions on shareholder value. *Total Quality Management, 19*(7–8), 777–791.

Papadakis, I. S. (2006). Financial performance of supply chains after disruptions: An event study. *Supply Chain Management: An International Journal, 11*(1), 25–33.

Worthington, A., & Valadkhani, A. (2005). Catastrophic shocks and capital markets: A comparative analysis by disaster and sector. *Global Economic Review, 34*(3), 331–344.
Zsidisin, G. A., Petkova, B. N., & Dam, L. (2016). Examining the influence of supply chain glitches on shareholder wealth: Does the reason matter? *International Journal of Production Research, 54*(1), 69–82.

Index

P. Schelp et al., *Supply Chain Disruptions and Stock Prices*, Palgrave Studies in Logistics and Supply Chain Management,
https://doi.org/10.1007/978-3-031-68885-0

The manufacturer's authorised representative in the EU is Springer Nature Customer Service Centre GmbH, Europaplatz 3, 69115 Heidelberg, Germany. If you have any concerns regarding our products, please contact ProductSafety@springernature.com

Printed and bound by CPI Group (UK) Ltd, Croydon, CR0 4YY

01/10/2026

02225983-0001